DARTMOOR
CENTURY

DARTMOOR CENTURY

Photography on Dartmoor Across a Hundred Years

Simon Butler

Contemporary photographs by
John Earle, Bryan Harper and Janet Bomback

HALSGROVE   HALSGROVE • DEVON BOOKS   DEVON BOOKS

PUBLISHED IN ASSOCIATION
WITH THE DARTMOOR TRUST

First published in Great Britain in 2000

Reprinted 2001

British Library Cataloguing-in-Publication Data
A CIP record for this title is available from the British Library

ISBN 1 85522 740 1

DEVON BOOKS
OFFICIAL PUBLISHER TO DEVON COUNTY COUNCIL

in association with

HALSGROVE
PUBLISHING, MEDIA AND DISTRIBUTION

Halsgrove House
Lower Moor Way
Tiverton, Devon EX16 6SS
Tel: 01884 243242
Fax: 01884 243325
email sales@halsgrove.com
website www.halsgrove.com

Printed and bound in Great Britain by Hackman Printers Ltd, Rhondda

Contents

The Royal visit to Dartmoor in 1909 at Huccaby races. On the right is HRH The Prince of Wales, later to become King George V. At his side is Princess Mary. On the far left of the pavilion, with his back to the camera, is Robert Burnard.

ST. JAMES'S PALACE

The essence of Dartmoor lies in its enduring granite landscape - obdurate and seemingly unchanging. It is easy to believe that such a place is immune from the ravages of time. Yet we see from the contemporary photographs in this book, mirroring those taken a century ago, that Dartmoor has undergone great changes. These images remind us that, despite its enduring nature, Dartmoor requires our continuous care and protection.

The Dartmoor Trust is an independent charity established in 1996 to grant aid practical projects which benefit Dartmoor, its communities and visitors. As part of its future role, the Trust aims to establish an archive of information, records and photographs for educational, recreational and research purposes. Based in a Study Centre on Dartmoor, the archive will be a major resource available to all and with worldwide access through the Internet.

The purpose of The Dartmoor Trust in producing this book, combined with the exhibition of photographs of Dartmoor "then and now", is twofold: the photographs remind us how rapidly those things we take for granted can change, while emphasising the importance of historic images in providing a glimpse into a past otherwise lost to us.

I am delighted to commend this book, and also the future aims of the Trust in establishing the Dartmoor Archive while continuing its excellent support of local endeavour.

ACKNOWLEDGEMENTS

The suggestion that the Dartmoor Trust might raise public awareness of its aims and purposes through an exhibition of photographs was the brainchild of Lady Kitson. It was she who gained permission from Lady Sayer for the use of Robert Burnard's photographs and who organised the initial selection of those pictures. For their support in this project thanks are due to the Sayer family. Lady Kitson was also instrumental in gaining the support of the Duchy of Cornwall for this project. The publisher gratefully acknowledges her enthusiasm and tireless support. Thanks are due particularly to John Earle, Bryan Harper and Janet Bomback who gave their time freely to photograph the present-day scenes complementing the Burnard pictures. Their work and that of all other members of the Trust is much appreciated.

The Dartmoor National Park Authority have supported this project throughout, not least in providing exhibition space at the High Moorland Visitor Centre in Princetown. Particular thanks are due to their Head of Communications, John Weir, whose cautious criticism, help and advice during the compilation of this book and in organising the exhibition was invaluable. Thanks also to his colleagues Kerenza Townsend and Mike Nendick.

Thanks are due to the other photographers whose work also appears in this book: to Stephen Woods for his images from *Dartmoor Stone* and Chris Chapman for photographs produced for his book *Wild Goose and Riddon*.

The works of many contemporary authors have been consulted and quoted. Thanks are due to them and to their publishers. They include Jeremy Butler, Stephen Woods, Eric Hemery, Reg Bellamy, Pauline Hemery and Peter Beacham, along with many others.

Peter Hamilton-Leggett, whose own Dartmoor Archive provides an example from which all other Dartmoor collections might be measured, gave cheerful and unstinting support, sustenance, and practical help. His is the photograph of Lady Sayer on the final page of the book.

Ian Maxted, Local Studies Librarian at the Westcountry Studies Library, as always provided much helpful and expert advice.

The quotation on the page facing the Introduction is from *Hole in the Sky* by William Kittredge, Vintage Books 1992.

Preface

BY THE CHAIRMAN OF THE DARTMOOR TRUST

The group of people who came together in the mid 1990s to discuss the idea of the formation of a Dartmoor Trust have always believed that it was important to proceed with caution; the objective being to lay down some firm foundations. Our shared vision has always been the creation of an organisation that will grow over a period of years to become a body bringing real benefits to Dartmoor.

Since its incorporation on the 12 June 1996 the Trust has invested wisely and used the income from this investment to support a wide range of projects across Dartmoor. In addition to this we have been working towards a major project: our vision for the Dartmoor Archive.

We believe that an archive which has both a physical base accessible to all and an electronic capability which will give it a world-wide dimension will be a widely used and much respected facility. The Trust is in the final stages of the preparation of a launch for the Dartmoor Archive appeal which will see a major drive for sponsors, the collection of original material, and the development of co-operative links with existing archives.

The Dartmoor Century photographic exhibition and accompanying book are vital steps towards the creation of an archive, providing as they do a reminder of things past and present. For an archive to be successful it must be a living thing, and the opportunity to record today in order to preserve for tomorrow images such as those in this book is of great importance.

I have been very privileged to be the Chairman of a remarkable group of talented and enthusiastic people who make up The Dartmoor Trust. It gives me an enormous amount of pleasure to see this project come to fruition and I congratulate all those who have worked so very hard to achieve it.

Philip R Sanders
Chairman of The Dartmoor Trust

"We think of photographs as a way of preserving the instant, defeating mortality and serving as a trigger for our most precious memories. But they also work the other way. We see people we have cherished, who are changed or dead, and we are reminded of our own fragility; photographs serve as doorways into the past and its stories, and as cautionary omens."
William Kittredge

Cottage Doorway. Stiniel near Chagford. August 1895. (Robert Burnard)

Introduction

Those ghosts that smile from old photographs once lived as real a life as you and I. Yet we look at them now with that same sense of separation as, when watching from a boat, we see figures on a distant shore; there is a but a brief moment of recognition before we pass by. One of the purposes of this book is to remind us that these early photographs are indeed our connection to the past - a real if fragile link to a time that no longer exists.

We live in an age in which visual stimuli invade every moment of our lives. Few of us can recall a time when television did not bring us news, entertain us, and sell things to us. Highly illustrated newspapers and magazines proliferate, while we take snapshots of almost every family event, and in turn are photographed without even knowing it by video cameras on street corners. We have so little regard for the photographed images in our family albums that few of us even bother to record what, or who, the pictures show.

Yet a little over a hundred years ago most people had no idea what their forebears looked like and photographs were truly one of the miracles of science. In many of the images in this book one can see how carefully people posed for the camera, and not simply because of the requirement to keep still during long exposure times. People posed as they would for a painting, often dressed in their finest, and looking their best. Photography was new, the equipment cumbersome and the process expensive; the chance to be captured for posterity came infrequently to most 'ordinary' people. Because of all this the quality of many early photographs is high; snapshots and disposable cameras appeared for later, less fastidious, generations.

Though photography and art have remained uneasy bedfellows, the exceptional photograph (whether through its 'artistic' content, or because it captures a dramatic moment in time) has always been prized. At what moment a photograph becomes important simply because of its historic value is less clear. Though pictures of our personal forebears have an intrinsic worth, at what point does almost any photograph become singularly interesting and worthy of collection? One answer may be simply that the image shows something has changed - something that was once in view no longer exists. On a philosophical level photographs are indeed a physical reminder of our mortality; more prosaically they are historic documents recording the passage of time.

Thankfully the work of many of photographers, such as Robert Burnard, has been saved for future generations to enjoy, and even modest collections of

Burnard's caption describes this scene as 'Watersmeet' formerly a public house - The Good Intent', Postbridge, August 1895. Although the people in the picture hold a pose, necessary if they were not to blur the long-exposure, the photograph contains all the elements of an intriguing story. The figure on the left is a postman, or possibly telegram delivery boy, while the man in the high-crowned derby (and with a steel sprig glinting on the toe of his boots) is reading a letter. Two women face the camera, the younger with a tiny sun hat perched on her hair. The plant pots and the large dilapidated mangle, plus the ornate box, the small wooden launder and the bucket suggest someone is moving in, or moving out of 'Watersmeet'. The house is newly thatched with a curious light let into the roof above the doorway which itself has a porch with a corrugated iron roof. Almost every old photograph bears some study with a glass although not all are as revealing as this.

historic images now achieve reasonably high auction values, often bought by local archives to add to their existing collections. Their value is increased if the photographs are largely related to a particular subject or location. It was not long ago that Victorian photograph albums were considered to be so much junk, especially if there was little indication of who or what the photographs portrayed. Thousands of early images must have been destroyed in this way.

The implication therefore is that photographs, along with many other everyday artefacts, are transformed from 'junk' to 'antique' simply by the passage of time. It is also true that the historic value of such photographs is considerably higher if (a) the subject is clearly identifiable, or (b) is described either by a caption (often handwritten in the album or on the back of the print), or can be identified by a living person. One of the essential tasks of a curator of a photographic archive is ensuring that this process of identification is carried out, and in preparing an index of images that is 'user friendly' to researchers. A look at any single county's Family History Society membership, and related sites on the internet, shows clearly the explosion in historical research at grass roots level, the result of a great deal of which is not far short of professional academic standard.

What is not clear, however, is who will take responsibility for the many millions of photographs in private hands that, although they may not be of national importance, form a vital part of the web of information that is encapsulated in what is known as 'local history'. For those involved in researching their family tree, or for community historians, such pictures are treasures waiting to be unearthed. All too often, however, as families break up, or move away from their native home, these photographs are thrown out, lost or dispersed.

The implications of this loss of a vital resource have been drawn into sharper focus during the development of the Halsgrove Community History Series, a project in which local communities are encouraged to produce a book describing the history of their parish or town compiled largely from photographs collected from within the community. It is often the case that a parish of less than three hundred souls will come up with around a thousand photographs

Lamerton School, West Devon, c.1925. Interesting in their own right, such photographs are of even greater importance to historians and family history researchers if the names of the children are identified. (From The Book of Lamerton, Halsgrove 1999)

Also from the Halsgrove Community Histories Series, the picture below contains a wealth of detail relating to farming practices now long in disuse. It shows George Ellis and John Brown at work on Foxworthy Farm in the 1880s and is one of a series of superb photographs taken by A.R. Hunt around that time. Again, what at first sight appears to be an attractive picture in its own right, also throws up vital information when further considered. (From The Book of Manaton, Halsgrove 1999)

and, though not all can be used in the book, they nonetheless form part of the collective history of the area. Much effort is made to identify the photographs, to ascertain the date, the event or location portrayed, and to name any people who appear. Often the oldest residents in the community will be called upon to help in this task and in many instances, through this activity, every child appearing in a school photograph from, say, the 1920s will have a name appended. But while some communities have already published a book, and others have such a project underway, there are many thousands in which the dispersal and loss of photographs (and those able to identify them) is a sad inevitability.

The impetus behind the publication of this book is to focus interest on the place of photographs in Local Studies and the importance of collecting and conserving them. On Dartmoor, that we have the photographs of Robert Burnard to help in this task provides an exciting and unusual visual stimulus, not least in the juxtaposition of photographs taken at the same location over a hundred years apart. These in turn, it is hoped, will help The Dartmoor Trust to raise the funds required for the establishment of the Dartmoor Archive.

We are fortunate in Devon to have a healthy number of established photographic collections: the Devon Record Office, the Westcountry Studies Library, the Dartmoor National Park Authority, individual library and museum collections and in private hands. For the first time, new technology would allow these to be drawn together into a single coherent resource, while allowing each original archive also to focus on collecting and archiving within specific subject areas. In the first year of a new millennium, with the dawn of a digital revolution on the horizon, the Dartmoor Archive project seems perfectly timed and entirely appropriate to Dartmoor's needs.

The industrial archaeological heritage of Dartmoor is revealed in a number of Burnard's photographs. This picture of the huge waterwheel at Whiteworks was taken on 1 June 1889. It also shows the massive stamps, employed in crushing tin ore, driven by the wheel, and the launder carrying water to the wheel. Such photographs are rare and but for them much direct evidence of mining practices on the moor would be lost.

Simon Butler
Halsgrove
March, 2000

The Dartmoor Trust

AND THE DARTMOOR ARCHIVE

Whether you visit, work, or live on Dartmoor you will appreciate many of the features which make it a special and much-loved area: stunning landscapes, important habitats for wildlife, thriving local communities, traditional land uses, and outstanding cultural heritage. All these qualities need to be protected, conserved and enhanced for the benefit of present and future generations. The Dartmoor Trust is a charity for Dartmoor's future. It helps to fund projects which conserve Dartmoor's wildlife and cultural heritage, support the social and economic well-being of local communities, and improve environmental awareness of Dartmoor's special qualities.

The Dartmoor Trust is an independent charity established in 1996 to grant aid practical projects which help benefit Dartmoor, its communities and visitors. Caring for Dartmoor costs an enormous amount of money. The Government funds some of this work, and other organisations look after specific sites. However, the extent and costs of such work far outweigh the funding available. Because the Trust's activities principally involve the giving of grants, its administrative costs are kept to an absolute minimum and virtually all money raised is spent on the ground. Together with local communities, we identify projects that need doing and that can be supported by Trust funding.

Projects already completed include the restoration of the bells at Gidleigh Church and the restoration of a Victorian water-wheel at a former grain mill in Okehampton; we have given financial support to the Devon Air Ambulance Service towards the purchase of an important piece of life-saving equipment and have grant aided the publication of a guide to the prehistoric site of Hembury Fort; by supporting the local community, a wildlife and recreation area on an island close to the centre of South Brent has been established and a derelict linhay repaired.

The opportunities and challenges are many, including repairing footbridges and stone walls, restoring important historic buildings, undertaking enhancement and amenity tree planting schemes, developing and improving community facilities such as village halls and youth clubs, providing improved facilities for people with special needs, encouraging research into Dartmoor's ecology and archaeology, and raising the awareness of Dartmoor's special qualities.

Recently The Dartmoor Trust has been working towards the establishment of a Dartmoor Archive. Utilising digital and internet technology, the purpose of the archive would be to encourage the study of Dartmoor through historic and

The Dartmoor Trust was formed in 1996 after the Dartmoor National Park Authority received a substantial bequest from a former lady resident of the moor. The bequest stipulated that the money be used for the good of Dartmoor. After much deliberation and consultation it was proposed that a charitable trust be set up, not only to make the best use of the original bequest, but to attract further donations, and by doing so to expand the work of the Trust.

The Dartmoor Trust logo is based upon the earliest known example of a silver penny which was minted at Lydford, Devon c.AD 973-5. It shows the head of King Edgar (944-975), younger son of King Edmund.

contemporary documents, maps, images and sound recordings. Such an archive would also encourage the conservation of this important aspect of our cultural heritage. The aim is to create a networked multimedia resource which would be widely accessible - whether in libraries, information centres, schools and colleges, or in the home. The Dartmoor Archive would perform a vital role in securing information about Dartmoor in a single archive and available to all.

Towards this end the Trust commissioned a feasibility study into the needs and requirements for the establishment of the Archive. The preliminary stages of this study were completed at the end of 1999. Identification of premises, funding requirements and the establishment of close liaison with existing archives and local authorities are currently in hand. The production of a photographic exhibition combining the photographs of Robert Burnard with contemporary images, is just one of the ways in which the Trust hopes to stimulate public awareness of its Archive initiative. Funds raised during the exhibition and royalties from sales of this book go towards the work of the Trust.

The Trust is dependent on private funds to help it support practical projects on the ground. It seeks support through sponsorships and from individuals who wish to make a donation large or small. Legacies and bequests are special ways of helping Dartmoor and funds from this source are being sought specifically for the Dartmoor Archive. Indeed, The Dartmoor Trust itself was established following a substantial bequest from a former lady resident who asked that her bequest should be administered for the general good of Dartmoor. Every legacy and bequest - no matter how large or small - will make a real contribution in helping Dartmoor's future.

If you require further information on any aspect of the Trust or its work please contact: The Secretary, The Dartmoor Trust, High Moorland Business Centre, Princetown, Devon PL20 6QF. Tel: 01822 890671 (email: dartrust@mwfree.net).

Robert Burnard

AND HIS LEGACY 1848–1920[1]

Robert Burnard, born 12 July 1848, was the son of Charles Frederick Burnard, Mayor of Plymouth 1881–82, and founder of the Plymouth-based chemical company Burnard, Lack and Alger, of which Robert was later to become a partner. Originally located in Sutton, the business was later removed to Cattedown where deepwater wharves were constructed alongside the company's warehouses. Robert Burnard was for many years Chairman of the Cattewater Harbour Commission, and it was from the harbourside workings that his interest in archaeology sprang. As Hansford Worth recorded in the foreword to his own book on Dartmoor:

Studio portrait of Robert Burnard as a young man.

The story of Robert Burnard's introduction to archaeology presents an unforeseeable chain of causes. His firm had waterside premises on Cattewater, in the development of which considerable dredging operations became necessary. The material dredged interested him and he enquired somewhat particularly as to its nature, deciding that it was such as might be yielded by the debris and waste from the works of tin streamers. His paper on dredging was followed by others on the streamworks of Dartmoor, the first of which he read to the Plymouth Institution on 22 March 1888. Always a lover of Dartmoor, his new interest quickly extended itself from the antiquities of historic time to those prehistoric.

Robert Burnard and members of his family, taken at Huccaby House c.1887. This picture forms the frontispiece to the first volume of Burnard's photo albums and is accompanied by a brief preface written in Burnard's hand: 'Illustrations of the wanderings of Robert Burnard in search of the antique, the curious and the picturesque on Dartmoor and it borderlands.'

[1]Part of this chapter originally appeared in *Dartmoor Pictorial Records*, Devon Books 1986.

Much of his early interest in the moor Robert Burnard inherited from his father, and together, in 1883, they were founder members of the Dartmoor Preservation Association. In 1891–2 Robert was elected President of the Plymouth Institution, and two years later, under the aegis of the Devonshire Association Dartmoor Exploration Committee, he began the systematic excavation of hut circles on Dartmoor. There followed, between 1894 and 1906, an intensive programme of excavation and restoration, involving both settlement and ceremonial sites, in which Burnard was joined by his friends the Rev. Sabine Baring Gould, Hansford Worth and J. Brooking Rowe, among many other pioneers of Dartmoor archaeological exploration.

Around this time Burnard's contribution to the Dartmoor Preservation Association publication *Plundered Dartmoor* has been described as 'as important to those who wish to preserve [Dartmoor] for the public, as are his antiquarian papers to workers in that field.' In 1911 Burnard was elected President of the Devonshire Association.

In 1972 the Royal Albert Memorial Museum in Exeter held an exhibition under the title 'Robert Burnard's Dartmoor – An exhibition of photographs 1887–1906'. In the catalogue, Patrick J. Boylan, then Keeper of Art, wrote:

> *The thing which distinguishes Burnard from many other competent amateur antiquaries of the period is the fact that in 1887 he began to use his undoubted gifts as a photographer in making a comprehensive record of Dartmoor – its people and places, its moods and scenes – and over the next twenty years a collection of more than 700 Dartmoor photographs was built up.*

A founder member of the 'Photographics', a Plymouth-based camera club, and later a committee member of the Devon and Cornwall Camera Club, Burnard's undoubted skill as a photographer is revealed both in the technical quality of his photographs, and in their striking composition. His use of these skills as a deliberate means of recording the Dartmoor landscape for posterity is part of his legacy preserved for us in his *Dartmoor Pictorial Records*, through which we

A number of Burnard's photographs record the work of the Dartmoor Exploration Committee which undertook the repair and restoration of several archaeological sites on the moor in the later part of the nineteenth century. Here George French and other labourers are seen 'finishing No 3 circle at Grimspound' on 26 May 1894. On the left is the Rev. Sabine Baring Gould.

Robert Burnard (reclining second from left) with members of his family and friends near Cranmere 12 August 1889. The caption reads 'we are all here except George French who was left behind at Mutes Inn to mind the cattle.'

have the earliest and most complete visual record of the moor available to us. Perhaps more revealing of Burnard the man are his family photographs preserved in the private collection of the late Lady Sayer. These reveal a kindly, engaging man, with a great love for his family and friends, and for the people of the moor. His photographs of family parties, picnics on the moor, and moorland walks with his family and friends paint a portrait of life far removed from the modern view of Victorian formality.

The photographs appearing in *Dartmoor Pictorial Records* and in this present work are, of course, mainly of the landscape. Where figures do appear they have the characteristic 'frozen' look typical of photographs where long exposure times required moving subjects to remain as still as possible. Some of the photographs will be familiar, as many have been reproduced elsewhere in a variety of publications. Best known, perhaps, are the pictures of the Princetown train snowed up in the blizzard of 1891, and the photographs showing the re-erection of the menhirs at Down Tor. Less well known, and perhaps more interesting because of the comparisons we can make, are the photographs of villages and homesteads on the moor, including an exquisite picture of the green at Meavy which has all the timeless beauty of a pre-Raphaelite painting.

In its obituary of Burnard, the *Western Morning News* remarked on the value of *Dartmoor Pictorial Records* with great prescience: 'The pictures are typical of the moor in its many phases, and the books hold an assured place in local literature.' Regrettably, the original negatives of Burnard's photographs are lost; many are thought to have been destroyed in the Plymouth blitz.

The first volume of *Dartmoor Pictorial Records* was privately published in 1890 in a limited edition of 150 subscription copies. A second volume of 200 copies appeared a year later, with volumes three and four following in 1893 and 1894, again each of 200 copies. Every volume carried a list of subscribers and was individually numbered and signed by the author and his publisher, William Brendon & Son of Plymouth. At the publication of the third volume, the author himself was expressing modest surprise at the continuing appeal for more volumes, though a glance at an original copy, its lavish binding and high quality of photographic reproduction, helps explain the demand.

Burnard's photograph of the snowbound Princetown train is one of the iconic images of nineteenth-century photography on Dartmoor. Burnard's own caption reads: 'The Princetown train snowed up on 9 March 1891. The weather side. On the left Mr Pudner, right Mr Nichol. On the engine Messrs Lakeman and Collins. Charlie has his head out of the rear window.' The photograph was taken on 14 March 1891.

Robert Burnard (standing second from right) and members of his family pose in their makeshift croquet pavilion at Huccaby House. The structure had previously done service as a Royal Box for the visit of the Prince of Wales and Princess Mary to Huccaby Races in 1909 (see page 6). Perched on the cross-bar of the pavilion, and leaning on her grandfather's arm is the young Sylvia, later to become Lady Sayer.

In his Introduction to the second volume of his work, Robert Burnard clearly states his aim in publishing *Dartmoor Pictorial Records*:

> *The preservation of Dartmoor is a subject in which all Devonians should take a keen interest. The railways which now encircle the Moor on every side are bringing each year larger numbers of roving holiday makers, intent on sport, the picturesque, or the curious. Whether this increasing popular appreciation is an unmixed blessing, as far as the romantic seclusion and solitude of this primeval region is concerned, may be questioned; but on the other hand, it must be granted that the more persons there are who take an intelligent interest in the matter, the more likely it is that this vast playground will be preserved for popular use and enjoyment.*

A number of Burnard's photographs included on the following pages also appeared in *Dartmoor Pictorial Records,* although many of them are previously unpublished. They are all taken from four large photo albums which, until her death in January 2000, were in the care of Lady Sayer. These albums contain around 500 photographs, some full plate size but many quite small prints measuring a few centimetres square. A number are now quite indistinct due to chemical reaction over a century or so. All contain a brief description in Burnard's hand, along with a precise date on which the photograph was taken.

Robert Burnard on the Banks of the Dart below Huccaby.

Computer scanning techniques allow even the poorest quality images to be reproduced and enhanced - although nothing has been done to change the image content of the photographs appearing here in any way. Burnard's original handwritten caption is included in the general caption alongside each photograph, as is the date he gives to each photograph.

The present-day 'matching' images are taken, as far as has been possible, from a similar perspective to the original. The name of the photographer is included in the caption.

Opposite: Robert Burnard standing in a ruin at Kingsett, 14 April 1888. His own caption reads 'a child amongst us taking notes.' He writes of the cavity at his feet: 'Not bevelled so it can hardly be a mould stone. It is undoubtedly connected with ancient mining. It is broken right across the middle.'

The Photographs

Lower Cherry Brook Bridge
Road over Cherry Brook bridge looking West - December 1887

Burnard stands on what is now the B3357 road between Dartmeet and Two Bridges, en route to Princetown. Hemery describes it as 'a small but finely built turnpike period bridge of two arches with a buttress on either side of the centre pier'.

This picture perhaps more than any other appearing in this book provides a graphic indication of why Dartmoor was considered a wild and inhospitable place, and how much it has changed in little over a hundred years. Here ragged rows of granite posts mark the edge of the unmetalled track winding its way up over the hill.

Lower Cherry Brook Bridge
The road looking west - January 2000 (Bryan Harper)

Today, many thousands of visitors, mainly car-borne, experience a similar, if more hospitable, view and may well stop here (a small car park can be seen on the right) to sit by the river.

The same road a little way on from Cherry Brook bridge. This is the Saracen's Head inn, now the Two Bridges Hotel, taken by Burnard in December 1887. The original bridge, now closed other than for access to the hotel, can just be seen in the middle distance. The road in the foreground sweeps down from the Moretonhampstead–Princetown turnpike, completed c.1792.

The Forest Inn, Hexworthy

The 'Forest Inn' Hexworthy - 9 October 1888

Few images could show so completely the extent of change in types of building on Dartmoor as this pair. Most early references to this Duchy property are somewhat disparaging and the soil pipes used as a makeshift chimney on the outside of the gable end give an indication of the rough-and-ready character of the inn (or more properly 'ale house'), although William Crossing describes it as 'a comfortable little hostelry'. Perhaps he was being diplomatic for it appears he spent some time here while compiling his classic *Guide to Dartmoor*, first published in 1909. It is said he even had a hand in painting the sign over the door. The barrels standing in the yard indicate the kind of hospitality on hand. Hemery in *High Dartmoor* writes that in the early years of the [twentieth] century the landlord of the inn, then 'not much larger than a cottage', was Frank Cleave whose grandfather had also been a tenant, in 1839.

Like so many of Dartmoor's thatched dwellings, the Forest Inn was the victim of fire. In 1913 it was burned to the ground, with only a small portion of the dwelling surviving.

The Forest Inn, Hexworthy

The Forest Inn Hexworthy - January 2000 (Bryan Harper)

In 1916 a new building was developed on the site of the former inn. With slate roof and rendered walls the new Forest Inn was out of character for a Dartmoor dwelling, and all the more idiosyncratic in that it incorporated a small remnant of the original inn. In later years the building was redeveloped with all vestiges of the original building being done away with.

Still a Duchy property, the inn today is a popular hostelry, particularly with walkers on the moor, thus retaining its links with Crossing who used to wake the landlord and his wife from bed on occasions when he returned, often after dark, from his ramblings on the moor.

Dunnabridge Pound

The chair in Dunnabridge Pound - 10 September 1892

Situated inside the walls of Dunnabridge Pound, by all accounts the chair is composed of the 'furnishings' of Crockern Tor stannary court, specifically the judge's chair (the seat) and the stannator's table (the canopy). Risdon refers to this court in 1630, while John Laskey, in 1795, suggests the relics were removed from the tor by a Mr Gullet of Prince Hall around 1780. The Rev. E. A. Bray in 1831 tells the story of the stone ('an arch-druid's throne') being removed by 'twelve yoke of oxen' to Dunnabridge Farm. And here the confusion lies:

William Crossing goes to some length to explain how the Farm has become confused for the Pound. Yet even he admits that most people would prefer a good story to the truth.

Whatever its origins, the structure was used as a shelter by the pound keeper who was charged with overseeing animals that were driven to the pound following the 'drifts' (a round-up of animals illegally depastured in the Forest of Dartmoor), and who then collected fines from owners. Anyone attempting to rescue their stock without payment of fine could find themselves impounded - locked up in the stocks which were sited within the walls of the pound.

The Reverend John Swete's watercolour painting of the chair at Dunnabridge was made on 16 January 1798. Records show that over 350 animals were impounded here on occasions, inside walls that were over five feet in height.

Dunnabridge Pound

The chair in Dunnabridge Pound - 1999 (John Earle)

Although the chair and walls of the pound remain remarkably unchanged over the century between the time these two photographs were taken, the striking difference is in the disappearance of Brownberry Farm just beyond the gateway. Both Hemery, in *High Dartmoor,* and Stephen Woods in *Widecombe-in-the-Moor* have photographs of Ada Coaker, whose father was the last tenant, driving geese in the lane between the pound and the farm in 1900.

Brownberry is just one of scores of Dartmoor dwellings that have simply disappeared in the last century or so. Changes in farming and the reluctance of families to put up with the exigencies of eking out an existence from the poor soil put paid to many such dwellings. Only in relatively recent times has the desire for 'country retreats', now fetching huge sums, saved many such dwellings from ruin.

Burnard's photograph of Brownberry, taken on 10 September 1892.

Spinster's Rock, Drewsteignton
Spinster's Rock - August 1889

Hidden in the shadow of one of the massive upright stones is Burnard's daughter, Dorothy. Spinster's Rock is perhaps the best known of all the chambered tombs on the moor, of which there are only a dozen or so. It was erected in the Neolithic period, around 4500 years ago. However, its seemingly obdurate appearance belies the fact that it fell down and was re-erected in the 1860s.

There is something rather satisfyingly prosaic in Burnard's photograph insofar as the monument is standing in a field of turnips.

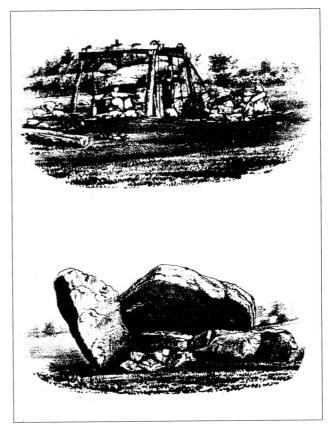

Spinster's Rock, Drewsteignton
Spinster's Rock - January 2000 (Bryan Harper)

Few people can stand alongside this monument without feeling something of its ancient power. It is one of the many archaeological sites on Dartmoor which exudes a sense of awe. In its original form the stones would not be visible as such tombs were covered with a mound of earth - a massive and impressive undertaking.

Early photographs of many of Dartmoor's archaeological sites, when compared with the present-day, show surprisingly little change. However, with large numbers of visitors to the moor each year potential erosion around some monuments is a cause for concern.

Drawings showing the collapse (in February 1862) and re-erection (in October 1862) of Spinster's Rock, Drewsteignton.

View of South Zeal

South Zeal - August 1890

As Burnard explains in the introduction to the first of his albums, his photographs cover Dartmoor 'and its borderlands'. Hence South Zeal and a number of other villages outside the boundaries of the high moor are included. In *Dartmoor Pictorial Records* (1891), he writes:

> *This picturesque village, in the parish of South Tawton, lies at the northern foot of Cosdon, or, as it is sometimes called, Cawsand Beacon. The village cross is a striking and interesting object, standing on a calvary formed of three steps of granite slabs, six inches thick, lying on square stones twelve to eighteen inches in height. The shaft is nine feet high, and the total height above the masonry is some sixteen feet. It was repaired about fifty-seven years since by a pious stonemason, who, when returning from America, was caught in a storm and vowed that if he returned safely to his native village he would put the cross in fair condition. Close by is the ancient chapel, dedicated to St. Mary the Virgin, and further down the straggling village are several old houses and inns worthy of notice.*

The repairs near to the head of the stone cross can be seen in Burnard's photograph. Even in August chimneys are smoking, woodsmoke from the cooking fires drifting down into the village.

View of South Zeal

South Zeal - 1999 (Bryan Harper)

This medieval 'town' is remarkably well preserved but although the major elements are still to be found in both photographs, there are any number of obvious changes apparent. In all the photographs depicting village scenes in this book the principal difference immediately noticed is the visual impact of the car. Take away the vehicles parked alongside the kerb in these photos and, even with the metalled road, the picture is transformed.

Samuel Prout's watercolour of South Zeal, made in 1806, shows the chapel and cross with a cottage between them, not apparent in Burnard's photograph.

The facades of cottages facing the street have changed little, although most have had their thatch replaced with tiles. The chapel of St Mary with its distinctive bell-gable dominates the market place, with the new clock face being the only discernable change. A recent undergrounding scheme carried out by the National Park Authority with the relevant utility companies has led to the removal of many poles and wires which detracted from the Conservation Area. This has helped restore and enhance the overall scene.

The Green at Meavy

The Royal Oak, Meavy - 9 May 1891

Burnard's reference is to the famous tree and not to the inn of that name which overlooks the green. In *Pictorial Records* he writes:

The ancient village of Meavy still retains much of its old-time appearance, for it possesses a venerable oak which Mrs Bray thought might have witnessed the Saxon Heptarchy, if not the Roman Conquest, a fifteenth century church dedicated to St Peter, with portions dating from a much earlier period, the remains of an Elizabethan manor house, a picturesque old mill, and a few interesting cottages. There is no doubt of the great antiquity of the oak, for although of big girth the timber forming the bole has quite disappeared, and the tree is supported only by a mere shell. It has lately been propped on the western side, and but for this support it must have succumbed to the blizzard gale of March 9th, 1891. It is to be hoped that the friendly hands which have thus far intervened to pre-serve this relic from destruction will continue to exercise such commend-able preservative influence. Under the shadow of the tree is the base of the village cross, with a granite post inserted, doing duty for the shaft which has disappeared. It would be a credit to the parish if a new shaft were procured on the pattern of that at Merchant's Cross [see following pages] *and inserted in the old base.*

The Green at Meavy

The Green, Church and Royal Oak, Meavy - 1999 (Bryan Harper)

In *The Book of Meavy*, Pauline Hemery provides a fascinating account of the tree's origins and the part it has played in village life over many centuries. She estimates its age as 960 years.

Writing about the green Pauline Hemery (wife of the late Eric), states: 'The village green was becoming ruined and growing smaller due to encroachment by traffic so in 1935 Mr J.R. Baker had the green enclosed by a low stone wall with fifty-five uprights in memory of his wife.' These are clearly seen in the photograph opposite.

Interestingly she writes 'the village cross, probably fifteenth century, was discovered by the rector, W.A. Gordon Gray, and restored by him in 1891'. This was the year in which Burnard took his photograph. In the modern photograph the village cross can be seen restored to its complete state.

Meavy schoolchildren gathered at the cross, 1909. (From The Book of Meavy, *Pauline Hemery, Halsgrove 1999)*

Merchant's or Marchant's Cross
Merchant's Cross, Meavy, 8' 2" high - 22 February 1890

In *Pictorial Records* Burnard writes:

An earlier photograph by Burnard, taken on 28 April 1888, shows off the impressive height of Merchant's Cross.

> *This cross, situated at the foot of Lynch Hill, close to Merchant's Bridge, Meavy, is the tallest and the best shaped of all the Dartmoor crosses. It stands a trifle over eight feet in height, with arms two feet three inches across, and fourteen inches deep. A cross is incised on each side where the centre of the shaft is intersected by the arms. It is most picturesquely situated, just within cultivated country, but on the very edge of the Moor; for the steep slope of Lynch Hill commences at its base. It was in medieval times the first guide-post for the wayfarer, who, if going across the wastes in a southerly direction, ascended the hill until the cross at Cadaford and that at Lee Moor, known as Roman's Cross, enabled him to reach the more hospitable districts around Cornwood and Ivybridge. If going east, it led to the village of Sheepstor, or by a route marked by nine crosses, over Walkhampton Common and the Forest, by way of Terhill and Down Ridge to Holne and Buckfast Abbey. Sometimes these pious symbols were set up as boundary marks in defining the limits of the Forest and the Commons adjoining. There is an instance of this in an Inquisition taken at Brent, A.D. 1557, when the bounds of Brent Moor were settled by jurors; and to make these visible and beyond dispute.*

Merchant's or Marchant's Cross
Merchant's Cross - November 1999 (Bryan Harper)

In his book *Dartmoor Crosses* the indefatigable Harry Starkey described a little over 100 crosses on Dartmoor while in his (unpublished) work Bill Harrison records 132, including a number that are now lost. There is little doubt that over the years many have been destroyed, used for other purposes such as in walling and for gateposts, or have simply fallen and become buried.

All seem to agree that this cross marks the Abbot's Way, although disputes have arisen over it being identified as the *Smalacumbacrosse* mentioned in the deeds of lands given to Buckland Abbey c.1280. A variety of theories are put forward for the derivations of the name Marchant or Merchant.

Pauline Hemery describes how, in 1937, the cross was 'knocked down by Mr Jury driving Bill Northmore's car when the brakes failed.' It was damaged again by a car in 1990. She also says of Marchant's Cottage (seen in these photographs) that it may once have been a hospice. No feature seen in the thatched cottage is recognisable in the modern building. Note how well wooded are the distant hills in modern times.

Langstone Moor Stone Circle

The stone circle on Langstone Moor - 16 October 1894.

A difficulty facing anyone interested in the past is in how far one is permitted to go in conserving and restoring important sites damaged by the natural ravages of time. Burnard and his colleagues on the Dartmoor Exploration Committee had few doubts that their duty was to restore these monuments. He writes:

The fine 'sacred' circle on Langstone or Launceston Moor has been hitherto strangely overlooked. It lies above the group of hut circles, opposite Greena Ball, and about one mile N.N.W. of Great Mistor. It was recently observed by the Rev. G. B. Berry, of Plymouth, who reported it to the author. All the stones, some of which are from five to six feet long, to the number of sixteen had fallen, but through the liberality of His Grace the Duke of Bedford the whole of these have been, this autumn, set up in the pits in which they originally stood, under the superintendence of the Rev. S. Baring Gould. The circle is 57 ft. in diameter, and stands on a stoneless moor, presenting a most striking appearance when approached from the north, with Great Mistor towering up behind it.

Burnard's photograph shows the circle following restoration.

The Rev. Sabine Baring Gould at Grimspound, 4 May 1894. He was a key figure in the activities of the Dartmoor Exploration Committee. He wrote a number of books, collected folklore and folk songs, and is celebrated as the author of the hymn 'Onward Christian Soldiers'.

Langstone Moor Stone Circle

Langstone Moor - October 1999 (John Earle)

This photograph shows the circle as it is today. Sadly much changed from its earlier aspect, albeit one that was much restored. In his *Dartmoor Atlas of Antiquities*, Jeremy Butler explains:

On a clear day the view from the circle sited just below the summit is exceptionally fine to the south and west but the monument has been sadly disfigured. All the stones were lying flat and undamaged prior to 1894 when the Dartmoor Exploration Committee re-erected them in pits still then visible in the peat. The circle became a casualty of World War Two when troops stationed nearby used the stones for target practice, fracturing ten and overturning others... Many of the shattered fragments lie around the site but it would be a considerable task to restore the monument to anything like its previous appearance.

The Church House Inn, Holne

The Church House Inn Holne - 28 December 1889

In the final volume of *Pictorial Records* (1893) Burnard surmises that the original building on this site was the priest's house. He writes: 'The present vicar, the Rev. John Gill, believes that this is the existing Church House or 'Tavistock Inn', which building therefore would date back to 1329.'

In the fifteenth century an upper storey was added and, later, the porch. In Burnard's photograph the arched window in the porch perhaps indicates its ecclesiastical origins.

Legend has it that Oliver Cromwell used the inn at the time of the battle of Totnes during the Civil War. The name was changed to the Church House Inn around 1800.

The Smithy at Holne, photographed in March 1892 by Robert Burnard. The poster on the door gives notice of the Weights and Measures Act while into the door itself are burned various brands, initials perhaps of local farmers. The railings in the background cover the mouth of a curious arched conduit. In past times the blacksmith was often associated with the village inn for he was sometimes also the cooper, making barrels in which to store beer and cider.

Note the tallet doorway in the right hand end of the inn has been filled in and replaced with a window on the ground floor. An open paved drain runs along the edge of the lane covered with granite slabs where it passes under the lane in the foreground.

The Church House Inn, Holne

The Church House Inn - January 2000 (Bryan Harper)

A number of Burnard's photographs are of moorland inns, including the Forest Inn, the Warren House Inn, The Old Inn Widecombe-in-the-Moor, and the Ring of Bells at North Bovey. Though many retain much of their original character others have been almost completely rebuilt. This photograph reveals that although the Church House has the aspect of a modern public house, almost all its major features date back to the earlier building.

At one time almost every community would have had its 'church house'. Often they were run by the churchwardens who would brew ale, raising funds for the church through its sale. It is known that the house at Holne was specifically to be used for the housing of visiting clergy, and when it became a public-house (the Tavistock Inn) is not known.

Note that the thatched building on the far right in Burnard's photograph has been replaced by a modern dwelling with a tiled roof; although the conformity of the structure suggests it is the same place.

Holne Village

Holne - 28 December 1889

The scene in these two photographs is so similar that one might be led to believe that time has passed Holne by. And it would be none the worse for that! Indeed Burnard writes in *Pictorial Records*:

> *Holne is still fairly remote and its parishioners have stood the civilising process without much being injured even though a railway has pushed itself within a very few miles of this parish. The ancient village revel is still kept up, for on old Midsummer-day a ram, provided by subscription, is roasted whole on Greendown Common, which overlooks the church and village.*

The vicarage at Holne was the birthplace of the novelist and essayist Charles Kingsley, perhaps best known as author of *The Water Babies*.

The Vicarage at Holne where Charles Kingsley was born in 1819. However the house shown in Burnard's photograph, taken in August 1892, was rebuilt in 1832 and, although it is said to contain parts of the older dwelling, it is probably quite different to the house that Kingsley knew.

Holne Village

Holne - January 2000 (Bryan Harper)

The immediate noticeable change in this photograph is the disappearance of the linhay on the left hand side of the lane. These open-fronted farm buildings were to be found on the majority of Devon farms, often with a line of granite pillars supporting the roof on the open side. This one has a tallet door in the gable end and appears to be such a substantial structure that perhaps it was taken down only because it served no useful purpose on the modern farm. Metal gates now close the break in the wall.

Although the wall on the right has lost its battlements and has been reduced in height, the remnants of the leat on the left appears to continue to wash mud into the lane.

Other than this the outline of buildings in the far distance appear little changed from a century ago, with the tower of St Mary's church prominent.

As in so many of these photographs it is interesting to note how many more trees there are apparent in the modern picture.

Holne Cross - a photograph by Burnard taken in August 1891. This cross was much restored in the mid-nineteenth century and is untypical of Dartmoor crosses.

Manaton Green and the Half Moon
Manaton - 13 August 1889

We see in Burnard's photograph something of the idyll that was English rural life at the end of the nineteenth century. It is high summer and the shadow of the young girl and the delivery boy, standing at the side of the green, is cast across the short-mown grass. Behind them stands the Half Moon Inn whose landlord at that time was James Harvey. The ivy festooned entrance to the inn was on the right of the building whilst the Post Office and shop entrance is middle left. With St Winifred's church standing just behind Church Cottage on the left, and the school to the right, Manaton Green formed the centre of this small community. Soon after this time Mr Harvey chose to build a grand house half a mile or so from the green, and this dwelling was later to become the Kestor Inn.

The hunt meet outside Half Moon on Manaton Green c. 1900.

Slinkers' Lane nearby, running from the lower part of the village but avoiding the green and the view from the church, was said to have come by its name given to those who wished to partake of the hospitality offered at Half Moon, without taking the risk of being seen by the rector!

Manaton Green
Manaton - January 2000 (Bryan Harper)

Though at first sight little appears to have changed in this scene in the passage of a hundred years, something of the gentrification of Dartmoor is apparent. The Half Moon is no longer an inn; gone is the ivy and the dysfunctional picket fence to be replaced by flawless white paint and neat wooden posts.

If for no other reason this circumstance exemplifies the value of photographs in acting as 'cautionary omens'.

43

Wistman's Wood

Messrs Lakeman, Pudner, Bullen and Burnie Headly in Wistman's Wood, Whitmonday - 6 June 1892

> *One aged wood*
> *Alone survives – the solitary wreck*
> *Of all those hardy foresters which erst*
> *Adorned, defended thee, and cheered the eye*
> *Of the old mountaineer.*

That part of Carrington's poem on Dartmoor concerning Wistman's Wood is typically eulogistic but the name itself could have come straight out of *Lord of the Rings*, so imbued is the name with mystery. Crossing suggests it may come from 'Welshman's Wood', and says that it is by this name that older inhabitants of the moor knew it. He also allows a possible Celtic derivation, as do others, of *uisg maen coed* - 'the stony wood by the water'. Early writers suggest that the placename might mean 'wise man's' wood.

Burnard's photograph of the bog oak is evidence that solitary oaks grew on the high moor where peat beds formed, but woodland such as that at Wistman's Wood was almost certainly confined to the river valleys.

Robert Burnard took this photograph on 22 August 1892. His caption reads: 'Bole of an ancient oak embedded in George French's turf tie. We hauled it out and found it to be 10'8" long, largest circumference (about 1' from roots) 3'4". From ground level [shown with arrows] to the bole was 2'3". On exposure to the air the wood blackened and became "bog oak".'

Wistman's Wood

John Earle at Wistman's Wood - January 2000 (John Earle)

The wood today has the same attraction as it did a hundred or more years ago. The dwarf oaks, home to varieties of xerophytic plants, grow up from the mass of boulders that strew the valley sides (boulders which saved the trees from destruction by miners according to Crossing). The site has been the subject of numerous ecological studies in recent decades - monitoring the effects of, among other things, grazing and air pollution.

Wistman's Wood Nature Reserve was established in 1961.

Haytor Vale

Haytor Vale - our lodgings for August 1896. From the right, Charlie, Mrs Preston, Mrs R.B., Mrs Hext, Lawrie B. Dorothy, Lawrie Headly. - August 1896

The scene is near the Rock Hotel (its sign can be seen at the far end of the row), where members of the Burnard family and friends stayed during one of their excursions. Although a smart new bicycle is in evidence it is likely that some members arrived by pony and trap (seen on the left), as a similar vehicle appears in other Burnard photographs.

The buildings in this smart row with their cobbled forecourts were erected around 1826 by George Templer. It was he who built the granite tramway which took stone (to build, among other things, London Bridge) from the Haytor quarries down to the Stover canal (built by his father). The cottages were to house quarrymen and their families, and the inn to provide recreation and lodgings for visitors. The inn had become a hotel by the time the Burnards visited, at which time the tramway had been closed for almost forty years.

Haytor Vale

The Rock Inn - 1999 (Bryan Harper)

Though it continues to let rooms the name has been changed back to the Rock Inn since Burnard's day. In other respects this handsome row of dwellings remains much the same. A century ago only one dormer window appeared on the roofline but the addition of others does not detract from the overall attractiveness of these houses.

Compare the wooded hillside in the modern photograph with the somewhat less bosky landscape above.

Jolly Lane Cot

Jolly Lane Cot, Hexworthy - June 1889

Within the National Park boundaries planning laws are under the governance of the Dartmoor National Park Authority. To the great benefit of the majority of those living in and visiting our national parks this position is to be welcomed. Against this background Jolly Lane Cot holds a special place in Dartmoor's history, as Burnard relates:

Jolly Lane Cot is an illustration of land cribbing from the Duchy by one of the small fry. This picturesque little cottage was erected in a single day [thus in law creating a freeholding from which the cottager could not be dispossessed] about fifty-five years since [in 1835] by the husband of the present occupier as a home for his aged father and mother.

The building took place on a day when all the farmers of the district had gone off to Ashburton June Fair (others say Holne Revel). The labourers of this district gathered together and 'on one day the walls were up, roofed in, and by nightfall a fire was burning in the hearth.'

Burnard's photograph shows Sarah Satterly (daughter-in-law of the original occupants) and her daughter at the door of the cottage.

Sarah (Sally) Satterly at Jolly Lane Cot

Left: *Sarah Satterly aged about 80. Born Hannaford. One of Baring Gould's singers. Lives at Jolly Lane Cot. Hexworthy - 2 September 1893.*
Right: *The window at Jolly Lane Cot - 1999 (John Earle)*

These photographs bear out the factual evidence surrounding one of the moor's oft told stories. As ever will happen such tales become clouded and doubts creep in (were the farmers at Ashburton or Holne?). Such images prevent confusion over detail consigning true stories, over time, to myth.

In collecting his folk songs around the moor the Rev. Sabine Baring Gould found Sarah somewhat problematic:

We found the sole way we could extract the ballads from her was by following her about as she did her usual work. Accordingly we went after her as she fed her pigs, or got sticks from the firewood rick, or filled a pail from the spring, pencil and notebook in hand, dotting down words and melody. Finally she did sit to peel some potatoes, when Mr Bussell, with a MS music book in hand, seated himself on the copper. This position he maintained as she sang the ballad of 'Lord Thomas and the Fair Eleanor', til her daughter applied fire under the cauldron and Mr Bussell was forced to skip from his perch.

Sampford Spiney Manor

Manor House, Sampford Spiney - 30 May 1891

On another of his borderland excursions Robert Burnard took this striking photograph of Sampford Spiney Manor. Devon, and particularly Dartmoor, is not blessed with many great houses and this manor is typical in size and aspect to many of similar date that are to be found on and around the moor.

This was the manor house of the Hall family and is now a farmhouse. The present building dates from 1607 although there was an earlier dwelling on this site.

Sidney Taylor's photograph, taken in 1939, showing the Manor court very much as a working farmyard, from the chickens and geese down to the anvil standing to the right of the low Jacobean archway. Such photographs are valuable in dating change and even in revealing differing economic circumstances between one era and another. (Courtesy Peter Hamilton-Leggett)

Sampford Spiney Manor

Sampford Spiney - 1999 (Bryan Harper)

Apart from refurbishments little has been changed. The roof was retiled prior to 1936 and the granite mullions on the first floor windows have been more recently replaced with simple square lights.

The major difference is the disappearance of the barn on the right of Burnard's photograph - a substantial structure. The similar building on the left survives, although the massive square granite trough has gone.

The granite paving slabs and handsome cobbles seen in the older picture, there to keep feet out of the farmyard mud, possibly still lie beneath the modern surfacing.

Cranmere Pool

Cranmere Pool. Visited 12 August 1889 from Postbridge by the following: R. Burnard, F. L. Burnard, L. F. Burnard, Olive L. Burnard, Charlie F. Burnard, Dorothy Burnard, Mrs Slack, Tom Easterling, Joe Reynolds, Frank Reynolds, Harold Williams, E. Bridgeman, J. Bridgeman and Charlie French. We took a horse and cart and five saddle horses as far as Mutes Inn. All our names were deposited in the cairn.

One would not expect to find much changed in these views of Cranmere - one of the most inaccessible places on the moor. At one time it was something of a mecca for visitors to the moor, a fashionable challenge enhanced by James Perrott, a Dartmoor Guide, who in 1854 set up a small cairn with a bottle where visiting cards could be placed (hence establishing the first Dartmoor 'letterbox'). Of course it is not a 'pool' at all, and Burnard writes: 'All who have attempted to reach the pool will concur as to its seclusion and utter dreariness... Its inaccessibility and its charm, and the fun of the whole thing is to get there, and when there to find it.'

EVENTS IN DARTMOOR HISTORY
(BY CHARLES LANE VICARY).

THE OFFICIAL OPENING OF THE POST OFFICE, CRANMER, BY THE MAYOR OF TEIGNHEAD.

A cartoon from a Plymouth newspaper of 15 June 1914 poking fun at the establishment of a letterbox at Cranmere.

Cranmere Pool

Cranmere - 1999 (Janet Bomback)

Something of the feeling of achievement on reaching Cranmere may be lost to the modern Dartmoor explorer, but it is still possible to share in the companiable experience of Burnard and his expedition members.

Members of the Burnard party near Cranmere Pool, 6 August 1892. Left to right: Charlie French, George French, Jack Bridgeman, C. F. Burnard, Stewart, Olive, Dorothy, Mother, H. Bowden, Lawrie B. and Lawrie Headly.

A Lane in Widecombe-in-the-Moor

Widecombe-in-the-Moor - 5 August 1889

Burnard took this photograph in the lane that runs up to Natsworthy, looking back towards the village centre and the church. People have appeared for the photographer dressed in their best clothes and posed, looking at the camera.

The scene, with the unmetalled lane edged with large granite blocks, is one of quiet rural charm, untrammeled by motorised traffic. The buildings to the right of the church are those clustered around the Old Inn. In *Pictorial Records* Burnard writes:

> *The glory of this quaint old village is the church which was erected some time in the fifteenth century, on or near the site of a much more ancient building. On account of the size and beautiful proportions of its tower it has earned the title of 'Cathedral of the Moor'.*

Burnard makes no mention of the Widecombe Fair, or of Tom Cobley, for which the village is best known today. This is somewhat surprising for it was his colleague the Rev. Sabine Baring Gould who first published the song *Widecombe Fair,* having collected it locally, and it was he who did much to promote the legend of Uncle Tom Cobley.

A Lane in Widecombe-in-the-Moor

Widecombe-in-the-Moor - 1999 (John Earle)

It is noticeable in a number of photographs in this book how road levels have been elevated over the last hundred years or so, presumably as each new layer of tarmac and chippings has been laid. This photograph reveals only the tips of the granite blocks appearing above the road verge, a difference in height of a foot or so from the picture above.

On roads never designed for vehicular traffic Widecombe-in-the-Moor can suffer more than many villages from congestion, especially in the summer months when coaches bring thousands to visit this famous spot.

It's also worth noting the electricity poles. It will not be long before these too become a feature of the past. Most cabling is now routed underground.

Headland Warren (Challacombe) stone row

The north end stones of the stone row at Headland Warren. Rev. S Baring Gould with hat off, Rev. Gordon Gray, Dr Prowse standing, Mr Wilder sitting - August 1893.

One of the instances in which it might have been better to leave things as they were. When, in 1893, the Dartmoor Exploration Committee began re-erecting stones in the row at what Burnard refers to as Headland Warren (now known as Challacombe stone row), they further obscured what was already a confusing position. Eric Hemery says 'Crossing mistrusted the restoration carried out some ninety years ago, not so Worth, whose one critical observation is that "a stone in the middle row was turned to form a blocking stone across that one row."'

Challacombe stone row

John Earle at Challacombe - 1999 (John Earle)

One of the best of the modern Dartmoor archaeologists, Jeremy Butler, in his *Dartmoor Atlas of Antiquities*, attempts to make sense of the evidence now available:

> *The rows were first reported in 1828 when most of the stones were found to be standing in their present positions, despite Crossing's remark that all were fallen at this date. A few within the row were re-erected by Burnard and Baring Gould in 1893, one of them probably set incorrectly across the middle row near its downhill end. Alongside this they also re-erected some fourteen stones in the haphazard position in which they were found making a very strange arrangement. Possibly these were the final stones from the lost north end of the rows, dragged here by the 'Old Men' excavating Chaw Gully who were always respectful of the antiquities in the vicinity of their workings.*

Note too that apart from the ground immediately surrounding the stones, heather is still the dominant plant cover.

The Ring of Bells, North Bovey

'Ring of Bells' North Bovey. Charlie holding Molly, next H. Headly, Olive, George Reynolds, Mother, Lawrie, Nora Bevill and Dorothy - 4 August 1894.

The original building is said to have been erected in the thirteenth century by stonemasons employed on the construction of the church, St John the Baptist, which stands on the opposite side of the green. This is by no means unlikely as such work would take months, or years, by a large group of men who would need somewhere to live during that time. It may, at this time, also have been the church ale house, brewing and selling cider and beer on behalf of the church.

The extension to the building on the right of the present doorway is fifteenth century. At a later date the building was used as a farmhouse and returned to being an inn, possibly in the early nineteenth century.

Friends and family at the Ring of Bells, North Bovey on 4 August 1894. Burnard's caption reads 'on left Lawrie B, then Lawrie Headly, Mother, Nora, Dorothy, George Reynolds, Olive behind Mother. Reclining Charlie on left and Hubert Headly on right.

The Ring of Bells, North Bovey

Ring of Bells, North Bovey - January 2000 (Bryan Harper)

Little has changed. A central chimney has disappeared and that on the right of the door but otherwise the inn, both inside and out, has escaped the ravages of modernisation. On the left the unrendered building seen in Burnard's photograph was turned into a 'stable bar' in 1967 by John Brackenbury, and its porch is glimpsed in the present day photograph. The Ring of Bells has had a long association with horses (racehorses were kept and bred here) and it is appropriate that a horse should appear in both old and new pictures.

Meldon Viaduct

Meldon Viaduct. A stormy evening - September 1890

On 12 October 1874 the London & South Western Railway Company opened a single track line between Okehampton and Lydford. The railway had to cross the steep sided valley of the West Okement River and this meant the building of a viaduct. By the end of the decade a second, adjacent track was added resulting in the construction of a second viaduct alongside the original. A close look reveals these two structures.

The two viaducts were ingeniously linked, and the lattice girders supported on five pairs of interwoven piers – the earlier piers are made of wrought iron and riveted together. The later ones are of mild steel and welded. Various strengthening improvements were made between the 1930s–1960s. The whole structure spans a distance of 163 metres and stands, at its highest, 46 metres above the valley floor.

Meldon Viaduct

Meldon Viaduct - 1999 (Bryan Harper)

In 1965 the railway was converted back to a single line, using the original viaduct. Soon after this the line closed but the structure remained in use as a head-shunt to serve Meldon Quarry. In 1970 a concrete road was laid across the viaduct to assist with the building of Meldon Reservoir. In 1990 the rails were finally lifted.

Meldon Viaduct is one of only two remaining examples of a wrought iron truss girder viaduct in this country and is a Scheduled Ancient Monument. During 1996 the Carl Bro Group supervised its refurbishment which included repairs to steelwork and masonry and the provision of new decking. The £650 000 contract was funded by CAMAS Aggregates (now Bardon Aggregates) and the British Rail Property Board. Its future maintenance and repair is now vested in the Meldon Viaduct Company Limited and the viaduct has been incorporated into the National Cycle Network benefiting both cyclists and walkers.

The effects of quarrying on the landscape are clearly seen in the present-day photograph where the huge spoil heap has encroached upon the shoulder of the valley.

Higher Merripit

Higher Merripit - 4 August 1892

Burnard's photograph of this extraordinary building provides a reminder of farm life on Dartmoor a hundred years ago. The great span of thatch, bedecked with lichen dried in the August sun, the huge natural boulders, give an impression that this is not a man-made structure but one that has grown out of the very earth.

Higher Merripit is one of the Ancient Tenements: farms within the Forest of Dartmoor which, due to their position on royal lands, were exempt from tithes. Burnard divides the tenements into two groups and writes that the occupiers of the Ancient Tenements possessed considerable privileges. These included being able to enclose land and, although there were restrictions on this, these 'newtakes' got out of hand 'so that almost the whole of the superior pasture ground of the forest is girded about by stone walls.'

Burnard's photograph, taken on 4 August 1892, shows 'Mr and Mrs Cleave and child, Higher Merripit.'

Higher Merripit

Higher Merripit - 1999 (John Earle)

Eric Hemery says of the house 'Higher Meripit (sic) Farm nestles under the south west foot of Meripit Hill; although a severe fire gutted the building in 1907, its interior rebuilding preserved many old features. More recent alterations have unfortunately concealed some of the still remaining architectural riches, such as a vast open fireplace, a fine clome oven and a granite stairway.'

It is difficult to believe these photographs show the same place, although the fire of 1907 explains much. Only the position of the chimney and the relative placement of the windows, to the right of the door, give clues to its former design. Nonetheless, the house is fairly typical of many Dartmoor farmhouses where a mixture of style and materials combines to form an interesting whole.

Grimspound

Entrance to Grimspound. George French standing in same. We cleared this and replaced the large stone at French's back - 28 April 1894

Along with fellow members of the Dartmoor Exploration Committee, Burnard began work on excavations at Grimspound on 31 March 1894. In *Pictorial Records* he describes the work undertaken:

> *The original entrance to Grimspound was to the south-east. This was much encumbered with fallen stones, which the Committee proceeded to clear out, when the entire entrance was revealed in its original condition, paved throughout, and with steps on the floor.*

George French, seen in the photograph, lived at the Greyhound Inn, Postbridge, with his wife and family. In his book, *Postbridge - The Heart of Dartmoor,* Reg Bellamy records:

> *George became a well known local character, being a leading Methodist, local councillor, and Justice of the Peace. He was born in 1852 and married Jane Ann Arscott, of Archerton, in 1878. For many years he repaired the road from Two Bridges through Postbridge and beyond. Along with Robert Burnard he re-erected many of the prehistoric stones in the area, including the two large circles at Grey Wethers. For this purpose he carted some 26 cartloads of stone to help trig up the stones they erected.*

Grimspound

Entrance to Grimspound - 1999 (John Earle)

The impressive enclosure at Grimspound is of Bronze Age date (c1700–600BC) and is the best known of the enclosed groups of hut circles on Dartmoor. According to the Dartmoor National Park Authority's *Guide to the Archaeology of Dartmoor* (1996) 'the enclosure wall is substantial and has an imposing gateway, which may indicate a more defensive character.'

The modern photograph reveals the effects of visitor numbers on sites such as Grimspound - notice the path that now leads up to Hookney Tor.

The caption to Burnard's photograph, taken on 7 September 1893, reads 'At Postbridge, Janie, Mrs French [Jane Ann], Charlie [on cart], George and Sarah'.

Postbridge

Greyhound Cot, Postbridge - August 1889

In his book *Postbridge*, Reg Bellamy (who, in 1954, became the tenant of the farm and the post office here) states that the Greyhound was built in the later half of the eighteenth century as an inn, with the first recorded innkeeper being Robert Valling in 1806. By the mid 1800s it was used as a farmhouse and, in 1895, also incorporated a rural sub-post office, with George French as postmaster. Bellamy writes of the picture: 'the photograph shows the house much as it was when originally built. Inside were open granite hearths . The upstairs floors were of plain oak boards. At the east end there was an outdoor open hearth, possibly used for smoke curing or some such purpose. Drinking water had to be fetched from a spring in Drift Lane and potwater came from the overflow from the duckpond.'

This photograph by Burnard, taken in 1895, postdates the picture on the left. It shows George French's wife and daughter sitting on the cart (on the backboard of which his name is painted). The lean-to has been dismantled by 1889.

Postbridge

Greyhound Farm - 1999 (Bryan Harper)

The modern photograph, and that on the right, reveals many of the changes incorporated into the Greyhound since it was first built. Some time after 1906 the thatch was removed and replaced with slate. The extension on the left end of the building was built c.1923 to house the post office and shop.

These changes are typical of many such dwellings on Dartmoor which have been remodelled according to changing times and circumstances. The pictures are important as documentary evidence of continuing social and economic change. For instance, in the past few years, some of Dartmoor's villages have lost their post office and village store, many of which have been in existence for a century or more. Yet who would have thought to record their passing?

A Chapman & Son postcard c.1925 shows the Greyhound as a farm and post office. The features built around this time are all evident in the present-day building.

Whiteslade or Snaily House

White Slade or Snaily House on the East Dart, looking down the river - 2 September 1893

The original newtake at Whiteslade appears to date from around 1700 and the eight acres thus enclosed from the moor is known to have been tenanted from that date until the 1860s. The legend attached to the dwelling, and one that gives it its name, concerns two spinsters who once lived here and who, it was discovered, supplemented their diet with slugs (called 'snails' by country people) which they boiled and salted down. In D*artmoor Forest Farms* (1994) Elisabeth Stanbrook provides a detailed history of the place and concludes 'That slugs were collected, salted and sold, and even eaten on the farm is plausible, but the romanticised tale is nothing more than that.'

Whiteslade or Snaily House

White Slade - 1999 (John Earle)

One of the tasks of the archaeologist and historian is to identify ruins such as those at Snaily House and to discover their origins. Legends and stories associated with a place, though of interest, can often mask the truth (folktales involving old ladies eating snails are associated with locations other than Dartmoor).

Photographs are unequivocal and provide firm evidence for the historian even when a dwelling has become ruinous. Burnard photographed many such places, particularly sites associated with farming and mining, and these pictures now provide a superb resource for those studying Dartmoor's past. The moorland landscape contains thousands of such ruins, from prehistoric hut circles to relatively recent structures associated with farming, mining and quarrying. Early photographs of these sites are worthy of preservation not least as, in time, the ruins themselves undergo change.

In John Earle's photograph of the interior of Whiteslade the huge granite lintel over the fire-place can be seen in the centre, with other interesting features to the right.

Ponsworthy

Near Ponsworthy - August 1892

Ponsworthy is a tiny settlement in Widecombe Parish, sited on the West Webburn River. These photographs show that, despite modern conveniences such as road signs and tarmac, the houses here have changed very little. Burnard's presence has drawn children to the doorway of the house, while the riders wait patiently for their picture to be taken. In the second volume of *Widecombe-in-the-Moor* Stephen Woods records: 'The cottages on the right are known as the Splash. Bessie French (nee Turner) now lives at No.2, and at the end of the second building is the forge.'

An early grist mill operated here, driven by the waters of the Webburn. It is first recorded in 1281 when it was known as Pauntesford.

This photograph by Stephen Woods shows the view from the opposite directions, with the forge in the foreground.

Ponsworthy

Ponsworthy - November 1999 (Bryan Harper)

Almost every feature on the Splash remains much as it looked a hundred years ago. All the window openings remain and only the porches over the doorways, one of them in corrugated iron, have been added since Burnard's day. In his superb book *Down the Deep Lanes*, Peter Beacham says of corrugated iron: 'It has entered the soul of the countryside in countless different guises and has long since proved it belongs there.'

The tractor, replacing horse power, looks quite at home.

The once open-drain across the road has been culverted.

North Brentor

North Brentor Church - 18 July 1890

Another of Burnard's excursions took him off the moor proper to visit North Brentor in July 1890. This church is not to be confused in name with that at Brentor, standing atop the magnificent tor, and which is dedicated to St Michael de Rupe. North Brentor's church dates only from the mid 1800s, as does its Church Hall which once did service as a National School, and can be seen on the left in Burnard's picture.

The church of St Michael on Brentor, looking north, taken by Robert Burnard c.1888.

The original image in Burnard's third volume of photographs is much faded due to the effect of two facing photographs chemically reacting. Modern scanning techniques can overcome some of the problems associated with faded images, and excellent results can be obtained where an image has sometimes almost disappeared from the original print. The conservation of historic images in photo-print or negative form requires expensive storage techniques using non-acid materials. Digitalizing photographs for computer output and storage not only allows enhancement but also preserves the image in a permanent and easily accessible form.

North Brentor

North Brentor Church - 1999 (Bryan Harper)

The present day view again has more trees evident. As with so many Dartmoor villages, electricity and telephone wires are festooned from poles on either side of the road – and will not be missed when eventually they are routed in conduits underground.

The old-style telephone kiosk, at one time considered something of an eyesore, are today granted special status in some villages, to be retained instead of being replaced with the more modern box design.

Runnage Farm

Runnage. Olive and Dorothy - 8 August 1892

'Rennage' is referred to in an early document listing the Ancient Tenements but, as Burnard suggests, the house here is not as old as those at Bellaford or Pizwell. Writing in 1893 he states:

> *Runnage is a modern house, built on the site of an old thatched erection which was destroyed by fire about twenty-four years since, and the tenement known as Warner* [Walna] *lies in Runnage bottom, further up the valley and nearer the Warren House Inn.*

Eric Hemery supports Burnard's reasoning 'the Ancient Tenement of Runnage formerly consisted of two tenements'. He goes on to speak of 'high drama' visiting the place when 'John son of John Stock' was murdered at Runnage in 1796. He continues: 'Since 1843 the Coaker family have occupied Runnage.'

Runnage Farm

Runnage - 1999 (John Earle)

Massive granite field walls don't serve the same purpose in modern farming and many have fallen into decay. Barbed wire is strung alongside the remaining wall in order to prevent stock straying, while wooden post-and-rail fencing can be seen in the fields in the background. The farmhouse and something of the original farm buildings survive and the whole settlement nestles deeper into the trees than in Burnard's day.

Buildings in front of the farm have disappeared and have been replaced by the wooden farm buildings on the right which is far more convenient for today's stock rearing methods. Indeed the practice of lambing out in the fields is now a rarity - just as the hayrick visible in Burnard's photograph is a thing of the past.

Sampford Courtenay

Before the inn at Sampford Courtenay - 19 August 1890

That this village should be the flash point of one of the country's bloodiest encounters, The Prayer Book Rebellion, in 1549, seems impossible when looking at its sleepy visage. The muddy ford across the lane, the tipsy wooden rails beside the granite walkway across the stream, and the old barn with its creased cob wall, together provide a picture of rural simplicity that would be hard to surpass.

Burnard himself provides no information on the little party that sit on horseback and in the little four-wheeled carriage, but we know that they went on to visit nearby Honeychurch church. Burnard took photographs of a number of the moorland churches thus providing useful evidence of the changes that they have undergone. For most it is the simple addition of a clockface, or perhaps rendering on a previously stone-faced tower.

Burnard's photograph of Honeychurch, taken in August 1890. Hoskins, in his incomparable history of the county, says of the church 'It lives up to its delightful name in a way that so rarely happens, and just to see it on a fine morning puts one in a good humour for the rest of the day.'

Sampford Courtenay

The Inn at Sampford Courtenay - 1999 (Bryan Harper)

The inn is recognisable instantly from its earlier guise having changed little over the century. However, all around it the scene could hardly be more different; the whole picture rings with a cacophony of visual clutter, overhead wires, sign-posts, street lights, TV aerials and telephone poles. Interestingly, however, strip these conveniences away and the essential fabric of the nineteenth-century village is still there. The white stone structure on the right, now roofed with corrugated iron, is the same little thatched building seen in Burnard's photograph.

Postbridge clapper

Postbridge clapper, Charlie and Dorothy - 22 April 1889

One of the best known and most visited of all Dartmoor's sites, the clapper bridge is also the finest example of this type of structure, common on Dartmoor. In his book *Postbridge*, Reg Bellamy provides a history:

> *Most writers suggest that it was built between the twelfth and fifteenth centuries. If this was so then the most likely builders were the occupiers of the Ancient Tenements e.g. Merripit, Pizwell and Bellever. The construction of the bridge must have caused some considerable problems for the builders. It might have been possible to find the granite blocks locally, but the slabs would most probably have had to be transported from further afield. Mr Jack Warne, who had expert knowledge of working granite, suggested they came from Lower White Tor, but an article in the* Western Morning News, *dated 16 May 1930, stated that 'The late Mr George French had located on the South side of Bellever Tor the actual spot from which the stones of the old bridge were taken'.*

Postbridge clapper

Postbridge - 1999 (John Earle)

The principal interest revealed from comparison of these two photographs lies in their background. The bridge itself, having withstood the centuries without harm, has changed little since Burnard's time. However, his photograph again shows how changed is the moorland topography since the nineteenth century. Almost without exception, the early photographs show bare hillsides on the uplands, often with the appearance of a 'managed' landscape. This is perhaps the legacy of the early 'improvers' whose crusade to farm inhospitable areas led to much enclosure on Dartmoor. Coupled with extensive newtakes, and the industrial development of mining and quarrying, these activities inevitably left their mark.

The present-day image portrays a much more wooded landscape around Postbridge, with the granite walls, now redundant, mainly obscured by scrub. It might even be said that today's landscape, in this photograph at least, appears to be more attractive – certainly less formal.

Bellaford (Bellever) clapper

Bellaford cyclopean bridge, by F. Reynolds. J. Shattock and R.B. on the pier - July 1888.

Another of Dartmoor's many clapper bridges, Bellaford has long since lost one of its 'clappers' - the huge slabs that sit atop the granite piers. This, sitting alongside the more recent three-arched bridge is a reminder of how vital were these early bridges to those who lived and worked on Dartmoor. As was pointed out in the *Ordinacio de Lideford* of 1260, the journey from the Ancient Tenements to Widecombe and Lydford was eight miles in dry weather, fifteen following a storm.

A Chapman & Son photograph of the old and new bridges at Bellever, c.1920.

Bellever clapper

Bellever - 1999 (John Earle)

It appears from the caption that the early photograph was taken by Frank Reynolds, a companion of 'R.B.' (who is seen sitting on the bridge), and who appears in a number of photographs in the Burnard albums.

The span across the East Dart River at this point was on the trackway to Widecombe-in-the-Moor (and thus on to the east) from Tavistock.

Reg Bellamy, in *Postbridge*, recalls the construction of a new road from the Moretonhampstead-Princetown turnpike road out to Bellever in the early 1930s. 'I remember there was a large granite boulder which had to be dynamited and all the Bellever children had to leave (school) early.'

Bairdown (Beardown) Bridge

Bairdown Bridge. The figures are C. Wotton and Bob Provis - July 1888

These two photographs and the smaller inset images are all from Burnard's albums. They represent Burnard's own 'before and after' pictures and are of interest insofar as they reveal how vulnerable were these early bridges to sudden and violent floods. Eric Hemery records its fate:

> *At the head of the gorge is Beardown Bridge, carrying the rough road linking the farm with the B3357. The bridge was built in 1890 to replace the previous structure of Mr Edward Bray, manager of the Duke of Bedford's west-country estates, who enclosed Beardown Farm in 1780 during the reign of George III. His bridge was swept away in the great Cowsic flood of 17 July 1890.*

Two photographs of Bairdown clapper bridge showing it before (on 7 August 1889) and after the flood of 17 July 1890. J. Brooking-Rowe in A Perambulation of Dartmoor Forest records that this clapper was destroyed by floods in both 1873 and 1890, each time being rebuilt, the second time by the Dartmoor Exploration Committee.

Bairdown Bridge

Ruins of Bairdown Bridge swept away in the flood of July 17th 1890 - 26 July 1890.

The small figure standing in the ruins of the bridge following the 1890 flood gives a graphic impression of the scale of the disaster. The same flood also swept away the clapper bridge on Bairdown, which is also recorded by Burnard. Of course when he took the original pictures, Burnard had no idea that the bridges were under threat, but he clearly recognised the importance of their destruction.

In the late 1890s occurrences such as floods and storms had a far greater impact on Dartmoor rural communities than they do today. In emergencies we can call upon various agencies to help out, but in Burnard's day people were pretty much left to their own devices. Heavy snowfall could mean isolated farms being cut off for weeks.

Along with the images on this page, Burnard took other photographs of the aftermath of blizzards, severe frosts, floods and gales. Such pictures are important records of weather patterns and changing climate conditions.

Cottage in Widecombe-in-the-Moor

The miller's cart with Dorothy and Georgie Slack - 5 August 1889

Another of Burnard's intriguing portraits about which one would wish to know more. The unhitched cart standing beside the thatched cottage implies this may have been where the miller lived. Apart from the empty shafts the canvas cover suggests the cart was ready for use and, with two horses to draw it, that the load was considerable (or the hills steep!). In his books on Widecombe-in-the-Moor Stephen Woods writes about the mills in the parish: 'There are possibly two in Widecombe, and others at Cockingford, Ponsworthy and Jordan, all within a mile radius.' He also identifies the girl in this picture as 'Dorothy, daughter of Robert Burnard, who married the Rev. K.A. Lake, curate to the Rev. Sabine Baring Gould.' We do not know who Georgie Slack is.

Cottage in Widecombe-in-the-Moor

Widecombe-in-the-Moor - 1999 (John Earle)

The cottage today stands on the road out of the village on the way up to the school. The granite collar on the chimneys is evidence of the earlier thatched roof although the outshot portion, with its half-weatherboard upper floor, has been replaced by a more conventional extension. The wall to the right has been tidied up and the gateway into the garden has gone. A small thatched structure in the garden has been replaced with a tiled building.

Down Tor stone row

Raising the stones at Down Tor stone row - 14 April 1894

This is one of a series of five pictures taken by Burnard to record the re-erection of the stones at Down Tor by the Dartmoor Exploration Committee.

April mists shroud the moor and the presence of the caped parson on the left imbues the image with an other-wordly aspect. Although not named, it is likely that George French is one of the workmen on hand, the clergyman being the Rev. W.A.S. Gray.

Whatever questions may be raised concerning the archaeological value in 'tampering' with these sites, it is clear that such is man's fascination with these ancient remains that they draw people like Burnard and his companions to them – as though to see the stones as they might have once stood is to divine more of their original purpose. That a churchman is on hand at most of these 'restorations' is perhaps no coincidence.

Down Tor stone row

Down Tor stone row - November 1999 (John Earle)

In the third volume of his *Dartmoor Atlas of Antiquities* Jeremy Butler provides a definitive view of the row and its recent history:

> *The spectacular row on Hingston Hill probably looks much as it did when the stones were first erected in Bronze Age times. Much of its present appearance though is due to Burnard and his associates who re-erected many of them in 1894. The majority were then lying flat, 'thrown down' about 1880 according to Baring Gould by 'men recently engaged on the row with crowbars'. The huge pillar* [seen in Burnard's photograph] *next to the cairn weighing about 3 tons had collapsed across its neighbour to the east. The sockets of the western three were excavated and deepened and the stones secured with 'a little Portland cement' around their bases.*

Drewsteignton

Drewsteignton - 26 August 1889

Burnard took his photograph of this charming scene twenty years or so before Julius Drewe, the millionaire grocer, decided to adopt Drewsteignton as his ancestral home. The castle he built nearby, the last to be built in England, and now in the hands of the National Trust, has since put Drewsteignton on the tourist map.

In *Pictorial Records* Burnard writes 'the parish westwards is only some two miles from Dartmoor, and claims a piece in these records as containing an interesting border village and one of the finest prehistoric monuments in the country [Spinster's Rock].' He goes on to say 'Flanking the village green are pretty thatch-roofed cottages with a good old-fashioned inn (yet dubbed the 'New') administered by the jolly Marks, as a good example of a Boniface as can possibly be found in a long day's march.'

Hoskins' statement in *Devon* (1954) that 'Drewsteignton village was formerly very remote, but now buses penetrate to it at intervals', is ironic in view of the present-day problems concerning the paucity of public transport available to rural communities.

Drewsteignton

Drewsteignton - January 2000 (Bryan Harper)

The fascination of these photographs is perhaps in that so little has changed. The stone cottage on the right has been rendered while the church tower now has a clock face (it is said the arrival of the Great Western Railway brought about the need for precise timekeeping in rural areas - before that knowing the time to the nearest hour or so would do).

Village pubs have so long been taken for granted that we often overlook their importance to the fabric of local communities. It is interesting that Burnard should comment on the publican of the New Inn, Mr Marks, for Drewsteignton, until the mid 1990s, celebrated having the oldest publican in the country. This was 'Aunt Mabel', Mrs Mudge, who had been at the inn since 1919. After Julius Drewe moved to his castle the inn became the Drewe Arms following a few years in which it was the 'Druid's Arms'.

After the death of Mrs Mudge there were local fears that the interior of the inn would be 'done up'. On this occasion someone decided the pub was fine the way it was - a decision Burnard would heartily have applauded.

Sherberton

The Ancient Tenement of Sherberton. Mrs Coaker and children in the doorway - 2 August 1892.

Along with Pizwell, Runnage and Merripit included in this book, Sherberton was one of Dartmoor's Ancient Tenements. Originally there were three tenements at Sherberton of which, by Burnard's time, 'the only house standing is that of Great Sherberton, a long thatched building of considerable age.' This is the dwelling in Burnard's photograph which is indeed one of the most attractive farmhouses appearing in this book.

The accoutrements of dairying - scrubbed pans drying on the grassy bank - the rake and bucket lying by the granite water trough, and Mrs Coaker and her girls sitting quietly by the farmhouse door, are silent reminders of an independent way of life gone forever.

Two further contrasting views of Sherberton by Robert Burnard (1892) and John Earle (1999).

Sherberton

The farmyard Sherberton - 1999 (John Earle)

Time has no regard for beauty and by the 1980s Eric Hemery is writing in *High Dartmoor*: 'Passing down the lane to the farm court, one is confronted, at least during the greater part of the year, by the activity of a successful riding establishment. The scene is backed by old Sherberton longhouse, now used for stabling and storage.'

Beneath the corrugated roofing sheets the essential form of the longhouse is still clearly discernable. The tiled porch and most of the windows and doorways allow the original layout of the house to be mapped with ease. Missing are the chimneys, at least that part of them extending above the roof line, and this as much as any other feature disguises its former use as a dwelling.

Even so there is much to be thankful for in this remaining as a thriving farmyard, keeping alive the continuity of the countryside. There is perhaps too much regard for preserving things as they are when the natural rhythms of life demand change.

Roundy Park Kistvaen

The great kistvaen at Roundy Park. Dorothy - September 1894

Kistvaens or cists, as the modern archaeologist would have it, are prehistoric burial sites. They are essentially granite 'coffins', made up of slabs forming head and foot and two sides of a stone box. A larger flat stone formed the lid and the whole was interred in the ground, originally covered with a pile of rock and earth. It is recognised that Burnard was the discoverer of this particular cist, as he records in *Pictorial Record*s: 'This, the largest known kistvaen on Dartmoor, was found by the author in August, 1893. It is situated close to the wall of the modern circular enclosure built of and on the site of a much older structure, known as Roundy Park.'

Burnard went on to excavate the site which revealed some pieces of flint, and burnt bone fragments.

Roundy Park Cist

Roundy Park cairn and cist - 1999 (John Earle)

Jeremy Butler lists 187 Dartmoor cists in his *Dartmoor Atlas of Antiquities* of which the cist at Roundy Park is acknowledged to be one of the largest. Roundy Park itself lies about a mile north-west of the clapper bridge at Postbridge. Butler describes the site thus:

> *It now stands clear of a much-denuded cairn, its size necessitating two cover stones and seven side slabs instead of the usual four. When discovered by Burnard in 1893 it had already been emptied and the contents piled alongside. Nothing was found among this rubble but he recovered two small fragments of flint and some burnt bones from the debris left inside. He also noticed that one of the end slabs was propped up on a 'cooking stone', perhaps one discarded from the settlement alongside. The cist has been slightly restored as Burnard re-erected two side slabs that had fallen and replaced one of the cover stones.*

That these two photographs show so little change to the site is heartening insofar as such artefacts appear robust enough to withstand the depredations of weather and people. It is to be hoped that the site will look no different after another hundred years.

Sheepstor

Sheepstor - 9 May 1891

This photograph reminds us that Dartmoor is both a natural and manmade landscape composed of granite. Early people made simple houses and even their last resting places from rough moorstone, while later moormen perfected the art of fashioning in stone almost every kind of object in which strength and utility were requirements. In this picture the eye moves from the rough wall in the foreground, where boulders are piled one upon another, to the cut stone in the wall bordering the road, then to the squared stone of the houses, and beyond to the church where are visible the highest achievements of the stonemason's art. Finally the eye is directed to the huge granite mass of Sheeps Tor punctuating the skyline.

Norsworthy farm, in Sheepstor parish, is another of Dartmoor's ancient farmhouses which today survives only as a ruin. This photograph was taken by Burnard in October 1894.

The churchyard contains a massive tomb of red granite where lies the body of Sir James Brooke, Rajah of Sarawak, who came to live at Burrator following an extraordinary career in Borneo. He died in 1868. His son, the second Rajah, died in 1921 and 'the grey granite forming the tomb was quarried in Sheeps Tor, and drawn down to the churchyard by eleven horses, and through the churchyard wall.'

Sheepstor

Sheepstor - 1999 (Bryan Harper)

Altogether a softer scene. Grass and shrubs have overgrown the sharp-edged granite walls. Stone posts mark the passage of the old stream where it is now channelled beneath the road.

The conservatory on the end house has gone but otherwise the scene is almost unchanged.

Lower Merripit

Lower Merripit. Said to be one of the oldest houses on Dartmoor - August 1889

The settlements at Merripit, part of the Ancient Tenements, take their name from the marshy or 'mirey' area from which a tributary of the Dart stems: the Mere Pit. Higher and Lower Merripit now straddle the cross-moorland route from Moretonhampstead to Princetown but originally must have been lonely outposts of farming endeavour, although Burnard records 'anyone at all acquainted with the neighbourhood will at once see that these ancient farms are seated in the best and most favoured portions of the Forest of Dartmoor.'

In *High Dartmoor* Eric Hemery states 'The fine old longhouse of Lower Meripit [sic] has one of the more massive porches', and goes on to list names of tenants, as does Burnard in *Pictorial Records*. These include the eponymous William de Meriput from the fourteenth century. It is known that the Bailey family tenanted the farm in the late nineteenth century, and it is possibly they who appear in Burnard's picture.

From the obvious junction between thatched and tiled building, it appears that the right hand end is a later addition to an earlier two-storey dwelling.

Lower Merripit

Lower Merripit - 1999 (John Earle)

Despite the many changes, there is a sense of satisfaction in comparing these two images. Both photographers have caught, in the people standing outside their home, a feeling of pride in belonging to such a venerable property (with horse and pig being included in Burnard's family portrait). It is sometimes forgotten that even historically important houses are, for the people who live in there, as much 'home' to them as any modern house. And it is people who make communities.

In fact, almost all the original features of the old dwelling remain. Though tiled, the roof line is detectably the same, as is the placement of chimneys (note the granite collar around the chimney which originally stopped rainwater running down the stack, throwing it on to the thatch). The doorway, far left, has become a window, but otherwise all the window openings are the same. The massive porch is also there, as is the doorway on the right, into the old shippon.

Wistman's Wood

Inscribed stone Wistman's Wood, with Lawrie and Dorothy - 19 April 1889. The inscription runs as follows. 'By permission of HRH the Prince of Wales, Wentworth Buller on September 16 1866 cut down a tree near this spot, it measured 9 inches in diameter and appeared to be 168 years old.'

Both William Crossing and Robert Burnard take exception to the ideas propounded by earlier antiquaries that Wistman's Wood, with its ancient oaks, was a haunt of Druids 'or that Druids reverently ascended them to cut the mystic mistletoe.' The experiment therefore undertaken - and deemed important enough to be recorded for perpetuity in stone - was to find out just how old these 'ancient' trees might be. As Burnard reports 'There is therefore good evidence that some of the smaller trees are not above two centuries old, but some of the larger examples are without doubt of much greater antiquity.'

Even a century ago there were concerns over the gradual disappearance of the wood and Burnard's photographs and writings are of importance to modern ecologists studying the woodland. Burnard describes the wood being separated into three distinct clumps: 'The middle group was seriously injured by fire in March 1885. This accident and the ravages of time are fast destroying this ancient wood.'

The Buller family owned the hotel nearby, at Two Bridges.

Wistman's Wood

Inscribed stone, Wistman's Wood - 1999 (John Earle)

Various moorland dwellers have shown a propensity for erecting inscribed stones or inscribing earthfast stones on Dartmoor. From early pre-christian stone crosses to the 'Ten Commandment' stones (1928) on Buckland Beacon, to the memorial (1991) to RAF crewmen killed when their plane crashed on Hameldown in 1941, there are literally hundreds of such artefacts within the moorland boundaries. The late Dave Brewer was the principal recorder of such stones and many are included in his work *Boundary Markers on and Around Dartmoor* (Devon Books, 1986).

'Incised stone at Sticklepath - Charlie and Bruce - August 1890' is one of a number of photographs Burnard took of early Christian inscribed memorials.

Though many of the inscriptions are simply initials recording a Parish boundary or a landowner's name, the stories behind these markers are often fascinating, and, where documents exist, tangible evidence of what might otherwise be dismissed as historical hearsay.

Crockern Tor Farm

Crockern Tor Farm, Lawrence - 26 December 1890

Boxing Day 1890 and Burnard is out with his camera despite the snow which lies on the farmyard roofs, blanketing the slopes of Beardown Hill. Apart from one or two flurries, snow is a rare visitor to the moor at Christmas these days, and the photograph is some evidence of how the climate has changed. In fact this Christmas snowfall was merely a precursor to the Great Blizzard of the following March in which Dartmoor was transformed into an arctic landscape. High winds caused the snow to drift, half-burying a train that had left Princetown that evening and uprooting a line of beech trees at Roborough (both recorded by Burnard).

Burnard's photograph records 'The storm of 9 March. The effect on Roborough Plantation, opposite the intake reservoir.'

Crockern Tor Farm

Crockern Farm - January 2000 (John Earle)

Crockern Farm lies above the West Dart River, alongside the track running from Two Bridges to Wistman's Wood. As Crossing describes: 'The path from Two Bridges to the wood lies through the enclosures of Crockern Farm, at one time known as Board'n House', a name which he tells us means 'wooden' house. In *High Dartmoor*, however, Eric Hemery disputes that this referred to the farm: 'I believe that the name arose when the wooden warren house was built above Wistman's Wood because, i) it was on the way to the Board House, and ii) it formed a headquarters for sportsman Saltroun when he wanted to shoot in the valley, when tenant Mortimore would ride up to the board house to let game-keeper Rooke know that "boss were comin".'

The present-day photograph shows a few changes. A thatched outshot building is now tiled, while stove chimneys protrude through the old barn roof on the right. The farmhouse is now obscured by a mature tree which quite possibly is the young tree in Burnard's photograph.

Mining on Dartmoor

Chaw Gully. Headland Warren, near Vitifer Mine. The figure is the Rev. S. Baring Gould. Looking east - 25 May 1894

Chaw Gully – 1999 (John Earle)

Burnard was a witness to the death throes of mining enterprise on the moor that had been present for centuries, yet had dwindled to nothing a decade or two after his death in 1920. Many of his photographs record sites and artefacts that have now disappeared, or have fallen further into ruin.

Chaw Gully is part of the activity around the Birch Tor and Vitifer Mine, known to have been active around 1750, worked throughout the nineteenth century, finally to close in the 1920s. Burnard in *Pictorial Records* describes Chaw Gully:

> *In places it is some forty feet deep and two to three hundred feet wide. In the bottom are several circular shafts lined with stone dry laid, which communicates with adits formerly used for drainage purposes. This is one gully among scores which seam the country in all directions and tell us how active in bygone times the tinners must have been.*

There is no better evocation of the final years of mining than in *Tin Mines and Miners of Dartmoor* (Devon Books 1986, 1994) by Tom Greeves who, recognising the likelihood that individual stories and photographs of the last days would otherwise be lost, set about collecting this material.

P.G.H. Richardson is another author with the perception to take photographs of mining remains and collect information. His book *Mines of Dartmoor and the Tamar Valley* (Devon Books 1992, 1995) is a treasury of images.

Although it is possible still to wander around the old mine sites on Dartmoor (with care - for shafts abound), most of the scars of this once great industry have gradually been healed by the reclaiming swathes of gorse and heather. Were it not for the photographs taken by Burnard, and others, it would be almost impossible to imagine how much of the moor was once an industrial landscape, laid bare, valleys echoing to the roar of water-driven wheels and the pounding of stamps.

Examples of Burnard's photographs of mining relics. Far left: Eylesbarrow mine blowing house 19 January 1889. 'This is the last of the Dartmoor blowing houses. In use 65 years since. Quite unlike the 'old men's blowing houses.' Centre: 'Gobbet Mine crazing mill - 7 March 1888. The back upper stone. Convex. The four holes are to take prongs carrying two or four bars, to work either by horse or man power.' Right: 'Erme Pits - February 1889'. This last picture is an indication of how badly disfigured was the landscape as a result of mining activity.

Claseywell Pool

Claseywell Pool - October 1894

Novelist, Eden Phillpotts, in *Tales of the Tenements*, writes:

> *There is a place on Dartmoor, on the great heath nigh Cramber Tor, called Crazywell. Here, Mother Nature, passing where old time miners delved for tin, has found a mighty pit, filled the same with sweet water and transformed all into a thing of beauty. Like a cup lies Crazywell upon the waste...'*

There are few river valleys on Dartmoor which do not bear the mark of tinning activity, spoil heaps, gerts and pits dug in the search for tin. Claseywell (spellings are various) is one such trial pit on Walkhampton Common. It has always been much-frequented and, before Burnard's time, had given rise to stories concerning its legendary depth. So bottomless was it that, even by tying all the bell-ropes of Walkhampton church together, the depths could not be sounded. Burnard himself put this story to the test and found the pool to be about twenty feet deep at most!

Claseywell Pool

Claseywell - 1999 (John Earle)

Only the clear footpaths and erosion around the edge of the pool suggesting greater visitor numbers differentiate these two pictures.

Eric Hemery suggests the pool is fed, and thus maintains a constant level, by an underground stream which then drains to Newleycombe Lake. Similar pits on the moor are also often full of water, even in the driest summers, and are evidence of the problems faced by early miners in keeping even their surface workings dry. He also describes the place, when wreathed in mist, as 'positively weird', and who has not found one or more of Dartmoor's solitary places a mite disturbing, given the right weather conditions and vague memories of one folk tale or another?

A photograph from the Hunt collection, taken c.1890, shows skating on the ponds at Peck Farm, Lustleigh. As with Claseywell, Peck Pits are a series of water-filled hollows resulting from mining activity.

Teign Head House

Teign Head House. The lonely house of the moor. Visited August 12 on our way to and from Cranmere - 12 August 1889

William Crossing in *Crossing's Dartmoor Worker*, writes:

> *Some of the Dartmoor farmhouses are lonely in the extreme. Teign Head, approached only by a rough track, has no neighbour nearer than Fernworthy, and that is at some distance from another habitation. Except during the summer when the rambler over the moor may call in at the solitary house, or when the moorman is abroad, there are no visitors at Teign Head.*

Teign Head Farm c. 1820, from a drawing by Samuel Prout (1783-1852).

Both Eric Hemery in *High Dartmoor* and Elisabeth Stanbrook in *Dartmoor Forest Farms* give a view on the establishment of the Duchy farm and newtakes at Teign Head, while J. Page in *An Exploration of Dartmoor and its Antiquities* supplies a graphic account of life at the farm at around the time of Burnard's photograph: 'It is a wild place and the bare-headed children - and there are always a small tribe of them in and around a Dartmoor Cottage - see so little of man that, after a prolonged stare at the stranger, they bolt into the house like scared rabbits.'

Teign Head House

Ruins of Teign Head farmhouse - 1999 (John Earle)

The farmhouse was requisitioned by the War Department in 1943 at which time its last tenant, George Hutchings, had to vacate it. Suffering some damage at the hands of the military the house was never permanently reoccupied and gradually fell into decay, eventually being demolished in 1971.

Another ancient Dartmoor farm in ruins. A Burnard photograph of Hexworthy Farm taken in August 1892.

Merrivale Hut Circle
Hut circle at Merrivale - 18 April 1891

The Princetown to Tavistock road sweeps out of sight down into the valley, crossing Merrivale Bridge over the River Walkham, to reappear as it climbs the hill past Staple Tor. Eric Hemery, in *High Dartmoor*, described the area from which Burnard's photograph is taken:

> *A large unenclosed hut-village of the Bronze Age south of the tor is bisected by the high road. This wide shelf of land from Over Tor to Long Ash Newtake is Long Ash Hill, where a population of some density once lived and farmed, probably at a later period than that of the sepulchral antiquities on the south tract of the hill.*

Of these 'antiquities', associated with the hut circles at Merrivale, Jeremy Butler remarks: 'Perhaps no other site illustrates better than Merrivale the limitations of present knowledge about the people of Dartmoor's past.' He follows this with a detailed study of this complex area. Of course Burnard's photograph does little to unravel the mysteries of our prehistoric forebears on Dartmoor and shows up the limitations of photography without supporting research.

Merrivale Hut Circle
Merrivale - 1999 (John Earle)

Little is to be gained by the comparison of these two photographs, except perhaps to note the absence from the modern picture of the telegraph poles that carried news from Tavistock to Princetown and onwards. We know that at around the time of Burnard's photograph wireless telegraphy was being introduced to even the most remote villages and towns, arriving at the Greyhound Post Office in Postbridge, for instance, in 1899.

In the distance can be seen the huge scar of Merrivale Quarry, opened in the mid 1870s and known as Tor Quarries. According to Crossing the granite extracted was said to be 'of particularly fine quality'. The quarry survived until the 1990s.

Nestling in the valley, next to the B3357 is the Dartmoor Inn - originally a row of cottages and now a popular and convenient refreshment stop on a well-used tourist route.

Widecombe Church and Church House

Almshouses, Widecombe - 5 August 1889

Widecombe Church is dedicated to St Pancras and, due to its size, is known as the Cathedral of the Moor. Earliest records date from the mid thirteenth century but it is likely to have been preceded by an earlier building. In any event the church as we see it today is medieval, with the tower itself being late Perpendicular.

The church roof contains a number of interesting bosses, including one depicting the Green Man and another of the tinners' rabbits (associated with mining in the westcountry).

The Church House, at one time thatched, was built around 1538 and possibly replaced an earlier structure. In *Widecombe-in-the-Moor* Stephen Woods describes the building as 'having two floors, the upper floors originally having been reached by external stairs which have now been blocked off. It also has a penthouse, the "pentice", a covered way on the opposite side of the stairs. For a great many years the village stocks were kept under the east end of the pentice.'

Widecombe Church and Church House

Widecombe-in-the-Moor - 1999 (John Earle)

Burnard refers to the Church House as 'almshouses' and certainly it was used as the Poor House in the early nineteenth century. In 1881 it was sold to the School Board, having been used as a village school supported by charity until that date. It is now owned by the National Trust.

Banish the cars and the overhead wires and the scene is pretty much as it was in Burnard's time – and for many years before that. Even so, seeing the buildings in their nineteenth-century setting brings home to us what, in its simplest form, the much overused word 'heritage' means: caring for things such as Widecombe Church House so that future generations can enjoy them.

Roof bosses from Widecombe Church contain symbolic figures such as the Green Man (top), and the tinners' rabbits. (Photographs from Dartmoor Stone *by Stephen Woods)*

Teigncombe

Teigncombe, remains of manor house - said to be former residence of Judge Whyddon - 16 August 1889

At first glance this old house appears to be occupied, with the children sitting at the front door. A closer look, however, reveals that the place is in the first throes of dereliction, and in use only as a farm building. Thatch is slipping from the eaves and the small leaded window panes are all broken. Weeds grow from the roof and walls. Where the little girl sits on a traditional wooden barrow the doorway is half bricked-up to prevent pigs (?) escaping. On the left, a boy stands outside a doorway framed with timbered door durns. He is carrying a pile of straw on his head. An 'evil' ('heave-ho'), a four-pronged mucking-out fork, leans against the wall. It is a scene of decay and poverty set against what was formerly a residence of some quality.

Another view of Teigncombe Manor, with a lady and gentleman framed in the distant gateway, perhaps the parents of the children seen in these photographs.

In *Pictorial Records* Burnard writes 'This picturesque old ruin is in the hamlet of Teigncombe, and was doubtless at sometime a superior residence. This house appertained to the ancient manor of Teigncombe, which is mentioned in Domesday.'

Teigncombe

The house in 1999 (John Earle)

In *A History of Chagford* (Phillimore 1981) Jane Hayter-Hames gives a full account of the Whyddon family: 'The manor of Teigncombe was held by the Bonvilles... and became the possession of the Whyddon family in the reign of Elizabeth I.' John Whyddon was called to the bar in the reign of Henry VIII, became a judge in 1552, and was knighted the following year. Described as 'a man of high stomach, and well read in the laws of the land,' he made a fortune from, among other things, the tin industry, and Teigncombe was but one of a number of manors held by him.

It is satisfying to see the old house sympathetically restored as a home, and with so many of its original external features retained. Though the thatch is gone, the worked granite and timber has been incorporated within the renovations. In this instance, a fascinating property with a long history, has been saved from incipient ruin.

Meldon Gorge

Entrance to Meldon Gorge - 13 August 1890

This view is taken looking in the opposite direction to the photograph of Meldon Viaduct shown earlier. Burnard's daughter sits in the foreground while the distant hills of Longstone and Homerton fill the horizon.

That so much of the moor has disappeared over the past century beneath vast expanses of water, or from the effects of clay mining, is a matter of regret, even when set against the benefits these industries provide.

In a world ever-shrinking, Burnard's photograph of a wild and solitary landscape is a stark reminder of what has been given up to 'progress'.

Meldon Gorge

Meldon Reservoir dam - 1999 (John Earle)

The massive concrete dam dominates this steep gorge. In Burnard's day the whole West Okement valley, running from Meldon to Sourton Tors would have been open moor. Little wonder then that the proposal in 1962 to site a new reservoir here met with considerable opposition, both from the National Park Authority and from local organisations such as the Dartmoor Preservation Association. Lady Sayer, grand-daughter of Robert Burnard was one of those who fought against the proposal while the plans meandered from one government body to another, eventually to find itself the subject of select committee consideration in both Houses of Parliament.

The scheme was put in hand, work beginning in 1970, with the reservoir beginning to fill in 1972.

Sampford Courtenay

Sampford Courtenay - 19 August 1890

A second view of this 'borderland' village, as Burnard describes it. What a different place this is to a moorland village proper. Compare this to the photograph of South Zeal, only three or so miles distant, or to Sheepstor, and one is immediately struck by the comparative softness of this scene. The walls of the cottages have a plumpness about them, with windows deep set beneath wide eaves of thatch. This is the edge of cob country, where the hard greys of the granite kingdom gives way to the brown soils of mid Devon. Here, houses on the left are stone built, on the right they are of cob.

The enemy of cob is rain, and further down the village, on the right, is a cob wall with a traditional 'roof' of pantiles. Beyond that are the conical roofs of thatched cottages – straw hats to keep out the weather.

Sampford Courtenay

Sampford Courtenay - 1999 (Bryan Harper)

A harsh critic might suggest there is not much to commend this view despite the fact that the major elements of the scene are unchanged. The muddy street has gone, of course, but so has the raised cobbled walk alongside the cottages - now given over to parking. The whole picture is dominated by the ugly array of poles, cables and aerials. Thatch has given way to more durable if less attractive forms of roofing.

Burnard's photograph would be a handy guide to restoration.

117

Pizwell

The centre house at Pizwell. George French on guard at the gate - 8 August 1892

This is known at the Middle House at Pizwell, a fascinating farming settlement in Widecombe Parish. In his book *Widecombe-in-the-Moor*, Stephen Woods identifies four farmhouses in this tiny nucleated settlement. The earliest reference is from 1260 and William Crossing says 'of all the ancient holdings on the moor none is perhaps so interesting as this small group of farms.'

George French, standing at the gate, figures in a number of Burnard's photographs. The French family figure among the earliest of its recorded tenants here, with John French making a newtake here in 1346. In 1635 William French of Pizwell complains to the Duchy about unfair tithe demands from the parson of Lydford. In 1839 a daughter was born to John William French at Higher Pizwell.

A second view of Middle House Pizwell taken by Burnard on the same date. Olive and Dorothy stand at the gate with their dog, while a bullock scratches itself on the end wall of the house.

Pizwell

The Middle House - 1999 (John Earle)

Roofing old Dartmoor dwellings made use of a variety of local materials: turf, bracken, reeds, rushes, heather, straw and broom were all used. Rye straw was considered best for thatching with wheat straw or 'reed' also being popular.

The majority of buildings in Burnard's photographs are thatched. This is no longer true of them today. As with Pizwell, the high cost of a thatched roof, its maintenance and insurance, makes it less desirable. It is said that the high nitrate content of modern wheat reed makes its less durable, more likely to rot.

Aesthetics come into it too, for the modern house owner likes a neat thatched roof, even where it may be patched. Burnard's houses often have holes and makeshift patching, and occasionally weeds growing from their thatch. As one farmer had it 'why waste fine weather mendin' holes that aint hurtin'?' Modern tiled roofs are not so attractive but are longer lasting and, once put on, cheaper to maintain.

The hipped roof has been replaced by a gable. Gone too are the pretty dormer windows.

Bairdown (Beardown) Man

Mr Pudner. The Maenhir i.e. 'longstone' stands 10'9" above the ground, is 3'5" wide on face and 1' deep. It is situated close to W. side of Devil's Tor and faces SSE - 11 May 1889.

This is one of four views of this prehistoric standing stone taken by Robert Burnard in 1889. In *Pictorial Records* he states that 'As a rule the Dartmoor menhirs are clearly connected with sepulchral remains, but Bairdown Man may be an exception.' He also suggests it has a connection with the Great Central Trackway, proving the existence of which was something of an obsession for his fellow Victorian antiquaries.

While most use can be made of historic photographs in identifying physical changes to the environment, it should not be forgotten that they are also of value to the social historian. Mr Pudner, with his little cap, three-quarter length coat complete with buttonhole, his pipe and blackthorn walking stick, is a far sartorial cry from walkers on the moor today.

June 1890 and two Victorian ladies are photographed by Burnard at Bairdown. Their high-button ankle-length dresses and flower bedecked hats must have been hostage to Dartmoor's difficult terrain and notoriously fickle weather (although, along with her paint-box, one has an umbrella).

Bairdown Man

Bairdown Man - 1999 (John Earle)

Many of the great monuments of the moor appear to have survived unchanged for centuries. This is in no small part due to the respect shown to some of them by early miners and enclosers of the moor who at times appear to have avoided damage to them wherever possible.

Jeremy Butler has compared measurements taken over the past century or so and suggests that peat formation has decreased the height of some monuments over the years.

North Bovey - The Green
Cross, North Bovey - 4 August 1894

The smoke from the chimneys of these North Bovey Cottages, even on an August day, reminds us that the fireplace was as much for cooking as for warmth. The object of Burnard's interest, however, is the village cross. In his unpublished work, *Dartmoor's Ancient Crosses*, Bill Harrison provides a detailed story:

> *During the Civil War the cross was thrown into a brook a short distance below the village, where it flows into the Bovey Brook, and at some later period it served as a footbridge over the stream. On 13 April 1829 an Act of Parliament was passed 'for the relief of Her Majesty's Roman Catholic Subjects', and whether this Act had any bearing on the salvage of the cross is not known, but in the same year the Rev. J.P. Jones, the curate of North Bovey, had the cross removed from the stream and set up in its present location on the green.*

Most writers agree that the cross and the socket stone in which it stands were not made for one another, with the plane rectangular shaft only half-filling the socket.

North Bovey - The Green
North Bovey Green - 1999 (Bryan Harper)

Here, the church peeps out from behind the cottage roof. Most of the dwellings here retain their original thatch, and few would argue with Harry Starkey that this is 'a perfect setting' for the old granite cross.

In fact the green is used annually for the village fair, a popular event that attracts many visitors. Indeed, Bryan Harper has done well to take a picture (almost) free of the cars which are usually parked around the green, often while their owners visit the Ring of Bells nearby. Perhaps it was after such a visit that the following occurrence, described by Bill Harrison, took place:

> *In 1951 a vehicle mounted the green and knocked down the cross and the Dartmoor Preservation Association advised the Parish Council on its restoration. Masson Phillips considered it was impossible to reunite the two broken pieces at the base so a new block of granite was employed and today the cross has the unusual feature of what appears to be a socket stone not much larger than the shaft, standing on an octagonal base stone.*

Thorn

Thorn, on the road from Chagford to Teigncombe - 16 August 1889

Like Teigncombe previously described, Thorn is one the ancient settlements of Chagford parish. Robert atte Thorn was known to have lived here in the fourteenth century and the family name of Thorn has survived in the area to this day.

The position of the site, at a right angle in the road, with the house facing square on to the highway is commonly found on Dartmoor. The implication is that the original track went *to* rather than *through* the settlement - an indication of its early origins.

Thorn

Thorn - 1999 (Bryan Harper)

The cottage facing the road, once two dwellings, has been converted into a single house, with an original doorway becoming a window. The desire for more spacious accommodation has seen this happen to many properties and, in this instance, Burnard's photograph shows what little effect it has had on the fabric of the old house. The old style of thatch, with hazel spars tying down the reed, has given way universally to a style where the spars are no longer visible. The modern thatcher also cuts around the upper storey windows whereas the older method provided straight eaves.

The house on the left has had a lean-to added, no small feat when the huge stones at the foot of the old wall are considered. The house next to it has had the thatch replaced by corrugated sheets.

Postbridge

Postbridge looking NE - the county bridge to the left - 10 October 1888

This view is looking in the opposite direction to the photograph appearing earlier in the book. As at a number of river crossings on the moor it is possible here to identify the development of travel on Dartmoor, from the original ford, to stepping stones, to the clapper and then to the arched turnpike bridge, well over a thousand years' span.

In his book *Postbridge*, Reg Bellamy identifies the ironwork from which poles were hung from the bridge to prevent cattle from crossing the river at this point. One of these poles can be seen in the photograph.

A Chapman & Son postcard showing the two bridges in the setting at Postbridge, with the Temperance Hotel on the right.

Postbridge

Postbridge clapper - 1999 (John Earle)

Trees have totally screened out the view of the buildings in the background. Note how few of them are species indigenous to the moor, although these are evident in Burnard's photograph too.

The building seen in Burnard's photograph is the Temperance Hotel, now the East Dart Hotel. It was originally built in 1862 by a tin miner, John Webb, who also farmed nearby. In 1863 a licence was granted for the New Inn but later it became a Temperance house. In 1909 the lease was owned by Solomon Warne whose great grandson is the publican there today.

*The Temperance Hotel c.1900.
From* Postbridge *by Reg Bellamy
(Devon Books, 1998)*

Dartmeet

Dartmeet - 8 March 1890

In *Pictorial Records* Burnard records that, in the Perambulation of 1240, Dartmeet is one of the defining points on the boundary between the Forest of Dartmoor and the manorial lands. He goes on to say that in 1689 it is first referred to as *Dartamet*, and continues:

> *The name was thus suggested more than two centuries since, and it is now perhaps one of the widest known spots on Dartmoor. It is right that it should be; for it is a lovely bit of moorland scenery, with just the picturesque amount of timber on the Brimpts side to contrast with the rocky and bold sweep of Yar Tor which rises between five and six hundred feet above the level of Dartmeet Bridge.*

He also records that, on 4 August 1826, during a violent thunderstorm, the clapper bridge here was washed away. It was later rebuilt under the auspices of the Dartmoor Preservation Association.

The photographs below are close-up sections taken from Burnard's photograph of 1890 and a photograph taken in 1999. They show the remnants of the stepping stones which once crossed the river at Dartmeet. Despite the torrents of the past century the stones have remained in place and unchanged.

Dartmeet

Dartmeet - 1999 (John Earle)

It is difficult to believe this is the same scene, and ironic in view of Burnard's comments concerning the 'picturesque amount of timber'. Although the bridge can just about be glimpsed through the trees, there is no sign at all of the distant moor.

Pizwell

Pizwell, formerly Pushyll - August 1889

Burnard's research into this settlement, one of the Ancient Tenements, left him in little doubt that Pizwell was among Dartmoor's more important farmsteads. He says:

> *It is probable that a portion, at any rate, of this old house at Pizwell dates from Bishop Bronescombe's time, thus giving it an antiquity of over six centuries. In 1300 3s.4d. was expended in the repair of the chamber of Pishull... and in the 10th year of Edward II, 13s.4d. was expended for the repair of the king's houses...'*

This Chapman & Son postcard is one of a number collected by Robert Burnard and Sylvia Sayer, and kept in an album along with some of his own photographs. Burnard identifies the picture as being the fireplace at Pizwell.

Pizwell

Pizwell - 1999 (John Earle)

Eric Hemery identifies the house on the right as being a longhouse, the original Higher Pizwell which was once known as French's Pizwell. The modern farmhouse is sited out of picture on the far left, built in 1922. The remaining two dwellings are seen in the centre of the photograph.

With thatch giving way to slate the modern settlement reveals a number of the elements that suit today's lifestyle, but the major features remain, including many of the original narrow window openings into the farm buildings.

Grimspound

No 3 hut circle Grimspound, partially restored, looking NNW - 28 April 1894

This is one of twenty-four circles identified within the walls of the enclosure at Grimspound by Robert Burnard. In 1894 and 1895 the Dartmoor Exploration Committee carried out extensive excavations at Grimspound, and Burnard, in *Pictorial Records*, gives a detailed summary of their findings. Having examined material taken from the interior, uncovering the hearth and the cooking hole, finding 'much charcoal' among the debris, the excavators decided to attempt reconstruction. Burnard writes:

Owing to the remarkable condition of preservation in which this hut was, the Committee resolved to reconstruct the walls where fallen, to bank them up with turf, and then to enclose the whole with iron hurdles, and to leave the floor exposed, with hearth, dais, and cooking hole, for the enlightenment of visitors.

Thus was created an early example of a Dartmoor tourist attraction.

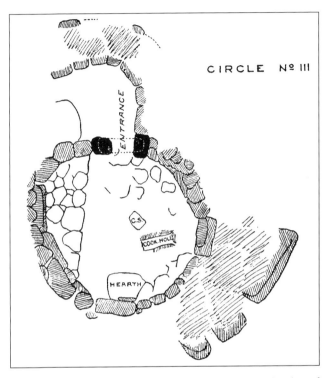

Robert Burnard's plan of Hut No 3 at Grimspound, from Dartmoor Pictorial Records, *1894.*

Grimspound

Hut circle, Grimspound - 1999 (John Earle)

Although the lintel has been toppled from its position the hut circle remains relatively intact. In fact the whole site has survived the passage of years and, in the first volume of his *Dartmoor Atlas of Antiquities*, Jeremy Butler explains some of the reasons why:

Until the nearby valley road was constructed in 1874 its remote position two kilometres from the Moretonhampstead to Princetown road ensured that it remained almost undisturbed down the centuries. Well above the newtakes in the valley no one has troubled to cart away the stones and the enormous slabs of the surrounding walls have been allowed to tumble slowly back to earth.

Note the well-trod path in the present-day photograph.

A panoramic photograph of Grimspound taken by Burnard on 19 May 1894.

Throwleigh

Cottage at Throwleigh - August 1890

The timeless nature of this corner of a quiet village is captured in these two pictures. Burnard's image in particular, with the two ladies in Victorian dress and the girl riding side-saddle on a Dartmoor pony, is a picture of rural perfection. Under the August sun it is almost possible to hear the sounds of the bees on the hollyhocks.

Throwleigh

Throwleigh - January 2000 (Bryan Harper)

It is remarkable that so little has changed. The cars intrude but the image is equally enticing. Note the thatched roof on the lychgate. This has prompted at least one 'expert' to enthuse over its Tudor origins when in fact it was erected within living memory!

Of the many images in this book, this is one that truly celebrates the constancy of the Dartmoor scene.

The Saracen's Head, Two Bridges

The 'Saracen's Head' Two Bridges. The figure is Mr Tweedy. December 1897

In *A Hundred Years on Dartmoor*, William Crossing describes the life of Sir Francis Buller who lived on the moor around the beginning of the nineteenth century:

> *The pioneer of those who endeavoured to introduce cultivation on a large scale into the district, was the first to look after the spiritual wants of those around him. Every Sunday worship was conducted at his house at Prince Hall, and thus for the first time in the history of the ancient Forest public religious service was held within it confines...'*

But as Crossing points out, Sir Francis also had thought for the corporeal needs of those around him: 'He also erected an inn at Two Bridges, since rebuilt, his crest - a Saracen's Head - being bestowed upon it as a sign.'

It is likely that the inn built by Sir Francis replaced an earlier ale house, originating c.1770, and said to have served traders at the potato markets held here.

The Two Bridges Hotel

Two Bridges - March 2000 (Bryan Harper)

Trees obscure much of the view visible in Burnard's photograph. The original arched bridge remains, although it now serves as an entrance to the hotel car park, with the main road sweeping by on the right.

The building in Burnard's photograph was badly damaged by fire in 1866 and rebuilt. In 1893, four years after Burnard's picture, a new building was constructed on the site and renamed the Two Bridges Hotel. This forms part of today's hotel which has been greatly enlarged and improved in recent years. It is appropriate to mention here that it houses a large collection of photographs of Dartmoor, among them the works of Chris Chapman.

A View towards Manaton

Looking towards Manaton from Smallacombe Rocks - August 1896

This view was enough to entice Burnard to stop, to assemble his heavy wooden plate camera, tripod and glass plates, and take this picture. It is worth reflecting, on how much effort was expended in Burnard's day merely in travelling to these remote spots. His family usually travelled in a little trap (seen in a number of photographs) with a pony in harness, while male friends and family went on horseback. Dressed as they were with Victorian decorum, and not always in fine weather, these 'excursions', as Burnard called them, must have been anticipated with some excitement, and not a little trepidation.

However, it is important to remember that for Burnard himself there was a serious purpose to his travels – his study of Dartmoor's antiquities. Nor should we forget that he and his colleagues were among the first to appreciate that Dartmoor was worthy of special care. As he writes, in 1891, in *Pictorial Records*:

> *The Commons of Devonshire extend like a deep fringe around the boundaries of the Forest, of which they once formed part... Yet these are in danger for proposals have been made to appropriate and absorb some of these commons. This must be strenuously resisted by all who have any desire to preserve intact these great open spaces of our county; for should an attempt of this kind succeed... this would amount to a national calamity and indelible disgrace to Devonshire.*

A View towards Manaton

View towards Manaton - 1999 (Bryan Harper)

At the time of writing the government has announced the building of a million new homes in southern England. That these two photographs show a scene – across this eastern edge of Dartmoor, to Lustleigh Cleave and beyond – that has remained largely unchanged in over a century, is due in no small part to those who, like Robert Burnard, have played a part in its preservation. Whether through the work of individuals, local organisations, or bodies such as the National Park Authority, such photographs portray the long-term effect of vigilant conservation.

Robert Burnard's photograph of 'Old George Caunter's Cottage at Dartmeet, July 1889'. Along with the rustic charm the picture contains a number of interesting features: the thatch under repair, the chicken coop outside the lean-to door on which are pasted notices of grass and livestock sales.

Dartmoor Photographers
and Photographic Collections

The bulk of archive photographs appearing in this book are those of Robert Burnard. However, although his albums are one of the finest sources of nineteenth century Dartmoor photographs available, he was by no means alone as a practitioner in those early days.

It is known that the father of photography in England, William Henry Fox Talbot, was taking callotype pictures in Devon in 1845, just four years after he patented the process. His pictures of the Royal William dockyard and the Citadel in Plymouth are some of the earliest known photographic images of the county. However, in those pioneering days, both the processes involved and the equipment required ensured that only a few practitioners were working. Not until later in the nineteenth century did it become possible for the amateur, usually one with a scientific bent and enough strength to carry the heavy glass plates and wooden camera, to indulge in the new art.

Fox Talbot's photograph of the Citadel in Plymouth was taken in 1857 and is one of the earliest known photographic images of Devon. It was taken just ten years after this pioneer of photography in Britain published the first ever book to be illustrated with photographs. From *Guns and Carriages*, Austin C. Carpenter (Halsgrove, 1999)

Burnard's entry into this field has been described earlier and, if he is pre-eminent as far as Dartmoor is concerned, he has had no end of disciples from that day to this. In this chapter a selection of the work of other photographers has been included along with examples of existing collections of Dartmoor photographs. The aim of this book is to stimulate interest in the establishment of a Dartmoor archive. Imagine what a resource it would be to have thousands of images catalogued and available from a single source!

As photography has become more accessible, and now with digital cameras on the market for a few hundred pounds, there must be hundreds of thousands, if not millions, of photographs taken on Dartmoor every year. In time these too will gain an historic value, but here we have space only to look at some of the existing archives and individuals who hold a substantial body of work. There are of course a growing number of photographers to whom the artistic element of the image is paramount. Practitioners on Dartmoor include Susan Derges, Gary Fabian-Miller and Carol Ballenger. This book is not principally concerned with this genre, although such photographers often also have topographical images among their work.

The photographers and photographic collections covered here fall into three categories: 1. Established archives in museums and libraries in Devon. 2. Photographers who have created a substantial body of their own work; those for whom photography is their profession, or at least an obsession. 3. Those who have made the collection of photographs of Dartmoor their interest, building up substantial individual archives either for private study or professional use. In all cases, this book is not intended to provide a comprehensive listing, but to draw attention to the spread of available resources.

Archives and Libraries in Devon

The Local Studies Librarian in Devon, Ian Maxted, has compiled an excellent guide to the resources of the county: *In Pursuit of Devon's History* (Devon Books 1997). This covers more than just photographic resources but its section on photographs is most useful. One must not overlook the value of other illustrative material, paintings and prints for instance, and these too are included in the guide. At the time of writing there are moves to digitalize the Somers Cocks collection of topographical engravings and prints, over 3500 views of Devon, including many on Dartmoor.

Hound Tor by Carol Ballenger. She is one of a number of contemporary photographer/artists who have produced images that are of significance both artistically and topographically. Her book Dartmoor Dreams *(Devon Books, 1999) and a current project,* Dartmoor Standing Stones, *contain many such images.*

Shaugh Bridge, Bickleigh Vale, from Devonshire Illustrated *by Britton and Brayley, 1832. This is one of several thousand topographical prints from the Somers Cocks Collection held in Devon County archives.*

Ian Maxted points to collections at the **Devon Record Office**, the **Westcountry Studies Library**, the **Beaford Community Archive**, the **Dartington Rural Archive**, the **Plymouth Record Office** (which holds a fine collection of photographs from the *Western Morning News*), and the **Torquay Natural History Museum**. The latter archive also holds the Laycock Collection relating to domestic and agricultural artefacts, including some photographs.

The **Francis Frith Collection**, covering a period from 1860–1970, includes around 15 000 Devon images, all of which can be viewed on microfiche at the Westcountry Studies Library (which also holds the Chapman collection), and at the **North Devon Athaeneum**.

Princetown c.1920 from a Frith postcard.

Devon County Council has a collection of contemporary aerial photographs, a number of which have been included in the book *Devon's Past: An Aerial View* by archaeologist Frances Griffith.

The **Dartmoor National Park Authority** too holds a collection of aerial photographs, along with a wide range of contemporary and historic images, including the Sydney Taylor Collection. Its contemporary archive, spanning some twenty-six years, contains a wealth of material recording on-the-ground projects, the effects of erosion, habitat changes, etc.

The Dartmoor Museum Association has an extensive photographic archive of north Dartmoor, held at the **Museum of Dartmoor Life**, Okehampton.

One of the thousands of images held by Halsgrove from the Community History Series. This shows a group at Leusdon School, Widecombe-in-the-Moor, in 1924.

143

The publishing company **Halsgrove** has, through the establishment of its Community History Series, amassed a large number of photographs of Dartmoor archived in a digitalized format. Wherever possible as much information concerning these images is held on record with them. For instance even the earliest of school photographs will include names of as many of the students as can be discovered, and in this way the collection will be of great assistance to those researching their family history.

Individual Photographers and Collections

It would be quite impossible to provide details of all those individuals who have contributed in this field and here we can provide a selected significant few. There were of course other photographers on Dartmoor before Burnard but few have left any kind of 'collection'. A contemporary of Robert Burnard, and also an author and antiquary, was **Arthur Roope Hunt**, a Torquay businessman who bought a farm at Foxworthy, Manaton, in the 1880s. His photographs and those taken later by other members of his family form a significant collection and were part of an exhibition organised through the Dartington Rural Archive who now hold some of his pictures.

Foxworthy farm, Manaton c.1885 - a photograph by A.R. Hunt. His pictures provide important details showing early farming practices.

Also important was the work of **John Stabb** who, in the early years of the twentieth century, published a number of books on Devon churches which he illustrated with his own photographs. Insofar as churches have not been entirely free of improvers, his photographs are useful when comparing changes wrought by man and by the passage of time. Although not every church on the moor is illustrated, his books *Some Old Devon Churches* and *Devon Church Antiquities* contain a number of important photographs. No single collection of his work is extant, although various prints and negatives are held in a number of Devon archives.

Another contemporary of Burnard was T. A. Falcon. Although he had more of an artistic than scientific bent, **Thomas Adolphus Falcon** (1872-1944), also produced books of his photographs of Dartmoor. In 1900 he published *Dartmoor Illustrated* and two years later *Pictorial Dartmoor*. He too was a member of the Devonshire Association and must therefore have rubbed shoulders with Burnard and his Dartmoor Preservation Association colleagues.

Falcon's photographs were deposited with the Devon Record Office after his death in 1944 and have now been dispersed into the general collections. He also issued a prospectus, in 1905, for a *Dictionary of Dartmoor*, but this was never published.

The priest's door at Throwleigh church, by John Stabb, from Devon Church Antiquities, *1909.*

T.A. Falcon's photographs of Huccaby Bridge (top) and Ponsworthy (left) from Dartmoor Illustrated, *1900.*

One of the biggest single photographic archives held in the Devon County archives is the Chapman Collection. Although many thousands of Chapman & Son postcards are in private hands, and are eagerly sought by collectors, this collection, deposited in the Devon Record Office (Ref 1578), comprises 3000 glass plates and 2000 prints donated by the Chapman family.

In the 1860s **William James Chapman** founded the most prolific firm of Devon postcard publishers. Based in Dawlish, in Regent Street, later in Park Road and Hatcher Street, the company became Chapman & Son in 1893. Although the firm closed in 1967, it was still possible to buy Chapman & Son postcards into

the 1970s from some Dartmoor outlets. As the holiday industry in Devon grew hundreds of thousands of their Chapman & Son cards must have left Devon bearing the message 'wish you were here' or its equivalent, for friends back home. There is no comprehensive published work relating to this remarkable family business, or to the Chapman Collection, but it would make a fascinating publication. Their Dartmoor images alone must run to many hundreds, a significant proportion of which have never been published.

Typically Chapman & Son postcards are in black and white and have the title and a serial number handwritten on the photograph. Their photographs are often not particularly artistic, and many show quite mundane scenes and events. However, in this lies their value today, for although pictures of the popular tourist spots are commonplace, Chapman photographs are often of locations off the beaten track. The Chapmans also took a series of pictures showing the last days of mining on the moor.

*Chapman & Son's postcards of the view of
Headland Warren and Hookney Tor (top)
c.1916, and the stone circle on Soussons
Common c.1911 (now of course, forested).*

Images of mining, farming and other industrial activities on Dartmoor are of great value to the historian and industrial archaeologist. These postcards from Chapman & Son show the buddle (top) and the stamps at the Golden Dagger mine c.1912.

A second major collection of photographs came into the hands of the County in the late 1980s. This was the **Sydney Taylor** collection, a cache of Dartmoor images that was brought to the attention of local archivists by Robin Fenner, the auctioneer of Tavistock. Through his care the collection was kept together and the glass plates, negatives and prints were purchased and are now held in the Record Office, with copies deposited at the Dartmoor National Park Authority headquarters.

Frank Taylor, Sydney's father, began photographing Dartmoor in the nineteenth century, passing on to his son his own collection of images, along with his passion for photography. Both father and son had an eye for the unusual, and a recognition of the importance of recording changes on Dartmoor, and thus the Sydney Taylor Collection is to the twentieth century what Burnard was to the nineteenth. Indeed, because of the number of photographs it contains it could be argued that this collection is even more significant and, were a Dartmoor archive to be successfully established, this would surely form the core of its photographic content.

Left: *Frank Taylor who pioneered the family interest in photography. Pictured here, with his camera, in 1923 at a hut circle on Ger Tor.*

Below: *Childe's Tomb photographed in 1947 by Sydney Taylor.*

Left and below: *Records of Dartmoor's industrial past: the mine stamps at Sheepstor, 1933, and quarry workers' cottages at Foggintor, Princetown 1942.*

Indeed, although the majority of the images were taken by father and son, they also copied old pictures and added them to their archive, and this makes the collection of further interest insofar as many of the original photographs they copied are now lost.

The photographs on these pages were kindly loaned by Peter Hamilton-Leggett and are images given to him by Sydney Taylor.

Sydney Taylor, 1937.

More images from the Sydney Taylor Collection (courtesy Peter Hamilton-Leggett).

Top Left: *The Warren House Inn, 1920.*

Above: *A view of an old house near the bridge in Horrabridge, 1934.*

Above Left: *Ruined cottage above Lowry, Burrator, 1935.*

Left: *Dismantling the Princetown Railway on Yennadon Down, 1957.*

John Stabb's photograph of Bairdown, taken in 1886. The end of that century closed a gate on a way of life that has gone forever. The barefoot child, the heather and straw thatch, the turf placed on the ridge of the rough shelter, are much the same as the roof over the heads of Neolithic man must have been, thousands of years before.

Collections in the Making

As photography became more accessible through advances in technology so more and more people were able to consider themselves as photographers, either as professionals or 'gifted amateurs'. From the 1950s and '60s colour film and slides became the popular medium and many of these early collections are in themselves of great value historically.

Eric Hemery, author of the monumental study, *High Dartmoor*, and other Dartmoor titles, has left a wonderful collection of colour slides, many of them taken during the 1950s up to the 1980s while he worked on his books. These represent a vital resource, as do the mono prints in that collection.

In more recent times, **Jeremy Butler**, author of the *Dartmoor Atlas of Antiquities*, spent hours flying over the moor taking photographs, and he too has a fine collection of colour slides. On the ground, his technique of taking a mosaic of photographs from a high tripod was specially developed in order that he could accurately plot hut circles, cairns and other small archaeological sites. The resultant photographs and related drawings will also be of much interest to future archaeologists.

Stephen Woods holds a particular place in the annals of topographical photography on Dartmoor for it was he who devoted forty years to capturing on film the thousands of granite artefacts, dwellings, and structures that are to be found on the moor dating from prehistoric times to the present day. The resultant book, *Dartmoor Stone*, has remained in print since it was published in 1988 and has established itself among the classics of the Dartmoor library.

Stephen Woods is also the author of two photograph-based books on Widecombe-in-the-Moor, the first compiled from pictures collected by his mother, Iris Woods. Both books have been published under the Halsgrove Community History Series.

Left: *The first photograph taken on Dartmoor by Stephen Woods, in 1948. This is a significant photograph in so many ways for not only was it the start of a magnificent project culminating in the publication of* Dartmoor Stone, *but it also is a reminder of the rapidity of change. There is today no sign of the buildings here other than an outline of where they once stood. Below are more photographs from* Dartmoor Stone *(clockwise from top left): monument base, Little Trowlesworthy Tor; Lee Moor hanging stone; trough at Headland Farm; granite roller at Nattadon Farm.*

A Chapman & Son photograph which later appeared in Tin Mines and Miners of Dartmoor, *Tom Greeves' superb study of the final years of mining on the moor.*

Photographs of miners and mining have always been scarce and much sought after. Other than those in official collections both **Tom Greeves** and **P.H.G. Richardson** have been assiduous in taking contemporary photographs and in seeking out historic images. **Owen Baker**, former county librarian in Devon also has an interest in this field.

At the risk of missing individuals who are worthy of inclusion here, the author is aware of many others who, either professionally or by dint of personal interest hold important private photography collections, large and small. Among these is **Peter-Hamilton-Leggett** whose collection of Dartmoor material in general is certainly the most comprehensive outside a professional archive. His publication of the *Dartmoor Bibliography* and updating of same has been a great boon to all researching the moor. His archive includes large numbers of prints and photographs, not a few of which he has taken himself over the years, and at one time he was 'official photographer' of sorts to the Dartmoor Preservation Association.

Those professional photographers who have published books or contributed to photographic books on Dartmoor include **Kenneth Day** (*The Dartmoor Scene*), **Peter Thomas** (*Images of Devon*), **John Head** (*Dartmoor Seasons*), **Roy Westlake** (*Dartmoor*), **Chris Chapman** (*Dartmoor - The Last Wilderness*, and *The Official National Park Guide*), **Lee Frost** (*Dartmoor*), **Carol Ballenger** (*Dartmoor Dreams*) and **Simon McBride**. All these have considerable personal collections and, of course, there are many, many others.

Newspapers and magazines often have their own photographic archives. **Elisabeth Stanbrook** editor of *The Dartmoor Magazine* has used her collection to good effect in a number of books and journals. *Devon Life* magazine and *Dartmoor - The Country Magazine* are also likely to build up useful collections over the years. **Paul Rendell**, editor of *Dartmoor News*, likewise.

Finally, this book would not be complete without the inclusion of the work of Chris Chapman. In recent times Devon has been extraordinarily fortunate to have not one but two photographers whose work combines the ingredient of historical record with incomparable artistic genius. The late **James Ravilious**,

A photograph by Peter Hamilton-Leggett of Wheal Betsy.

is known mainly for the work he produced in and around Mid and North Devon. His work for the Beaford Community Archive has left a superb legacy in the form of hundreds of photographs, both his own and historic images. He also worked on Dartmoor, sometimes with his close friend Chris Chapman. Although their style is quite individual, these two photographers have created between them bodies of work that will long remain the envy of other regional collections in Britain.

In 1999, supported by the Dartmoor Trust and sponsored by other groups, organisations and individuals, Chris Chapman spent a year completing the work on his highly acclaimed book *Wild Goose and Riddon,* published in October 2000. The book is a major contribution to photography on the moor at the start of the new millennium, and timely, as the Dartmoor Trust itself moves towards achieving its ambition of establishing an archive for Dartmoor.

Chris Chapman's son, Jed, at Spinster's Rock, 1999.

Owen and Joe White at Batworthy Farm - Chris Chapman.

Bibliography

AND FURTHER READING

Atkinson et al. *Dartmoor Mines of the Granite Mass,* Exeter 1978

Baldwin et al. *The Book of Manaton,* Halsgrove 1999

Bellamy, Reg. *The Book of Postbridge,* Devon Books 1998

Brears, Peter. *The Old Devon Farmhouse,* Devon Books 1998

Brewer, D. *Field Guide to Boundary Markers on Dartmoor,* Devon Books 1986

Britton and Brayley. *Devonshire Illustrated,* London 1832

Burnard, Robert. *Dartmoor Pictorial Records,* Devon Books 1986

Butler, Jeremy. *Dartmoor Atlas of Antiquities* Vols 1–5, Devon Books 1991-97

Butler, Simon. *A Gentleman's Walking Tor of Dartmoor,* Devon Books 1986

Carter, B. & Skilton B. *Dartmoor: Threatened Wilderness.* Channel 4 1987

Cherry, B. and Pevsner N. *The Buildings of England: Devon,* Penguin 1989

Chugg, Brian. *Victorian and Edwardian Devon,* Batsford 1979

Crossing, William. *Ancient Stone Crosses of Dartmoor,* Devon Books 1987

Crossing, William. *Dartmoor Worker,* Peninsula Press 1992

Crossing, William. *Gems in a Granite Setting,* Devon Books 1987

Crossing, William. *Guide to Dartmoor,* Peninsula Press 1990

Crossing, William. *One Hundred Years on Dartmoor,* Devon Books 1987

Dartmoor National Park Authority. *Guide to Archaeology,* Devon Books 1996

Dartmoor Preservation Association. *A Dartmoor Century,* DPA 1983

Day, Kenneth F. *The Dartmoor Scene,* Frederick Muller 1946

Day, Kenneth F. *Days on Dartmoor,* Devon Books 1987

Fenner, Robin A. *Devon and Cornwall Illustrated,* Stannary Press 1986

Frost, Lee & Robinson Ian. *Dartmoor,* Colin Baxter 1999

Gawne, E. & Sanders, J. *Early Dartmoor Farmhouses,* Orchard 1998

Gill, Crispin. *Dartmoor: A New Study,* David & Charles 1983

Gray, T. & Rowe, M. *Travels in Georgian Devon* Vol III, Devon Books 1999

Greeves, Tom. *Tin Mines and Miners of Dartmoor,* Devon Books 1986

Griffith, Frances. *Devon's Past: An Aerial View,* Devon Books 1988

Hamilton-Leggett, Peter. *The Dartmoor Bibliography,* Devon Books 1992

Harris, Colin. *Stowford Papermill,* Halsgrove 1999

Harrison, W. *Dartmoor Ancient Crosses.* Unpubl.mss

Hemery, Eric. *High Dartmoor*, Robert Hale 1983

Hemery, Pauline. *The Book of Meavy*, Halsgrove 1999

Hoskins, W.G. *Devon*, Devon Books 1992

Lauder, Rosemary Anne. *Views of Old Devon,* Bossiney Books 1982

Maxted, Ian (Ed.). *In Pursuit of Devon's History*, Devon Books 1997

Mildren, James. *Dartmoor in the Old Days,* Bossiney Books 1984

Needham, David. *Francis Frith's Devon,* Frith Book Co. 1999

Prince, E. & Head J. *Dartmoor Seasons,* Devon Books 1987

Quick, Tom. *Dartmoor Inns,* Devon Books 1992

Randall-Page, P. & Chapman C. *Granite Song,* Devon Books 1999

Richardson, P.H.G. *Mines of Dartmoor and the Tamar Valley*, Devon Books 1995

Rowe, Samuel. *A Perambulation of Dartmoor*, Devon Books 1985

Sayer, Sylvia. *The Outline of Dartmoor's Story,* Devon Books 1988

Smiles, S. & Pidgley, M. *The Perfection of England*, Exeter 1995

Smith, Martin. *The Railways of Devon,* Ian Allan 1993

Stabb, John. *Devon Church Antiquities*, Simpkin & Marshall 1909

Stanbrook, Elisabeth. *Dartmoor Forest Farms,* Devon Books 1994

Stanes, Robin. *The Old Farm,* Devon Books 1990

Starkey, Harry. *Dartmoor Crosses,* Starkey 1989

Thomas, Peter. *Images of Devon,* Halsgrove 1999

Westlake, Roy. *Dartmoor,* David & Charles 1987

Woods, Stephen. *Dartmoor Stone,* Devon Books 1999

Woods, Stephen. *Widecombe - A Pictorial History*, Devon Books 1996

Woods, Stephen *Widecombe - Uncle Tom Cobley and All,* Devon Books 2000

Index of Photographs

REFERRING TO THE BURNARD PHOTOGRAPHS IN THE MAIN BODY OF THE BOOK

Dedicated to the memory of
Sylvia Sayer

1904–2000